JANE EYRE

AN ADAPTED CLASSIC

Jane Eyre

CHARLOTTE BRONTË

GLOBE FEARON
Pearson Learning Group

JEROME CARLIN

former Director of English, K–12
New York City Public Schools

HENRY I. CHRIST

former Vice-President,
New York State English Council, and
former Director of the National Council
of Teachers of English

M. JERRY WEISS

Distinguished Service Professor of Communication
Jersey City State College
Jersey City, New Jersey

Cover design: Marek Antoniak
Cover illustration: Natalie Grenschenko

ISBN 0-8359-0215-3
Printed in the United States of America
10 11 12 13 14   07 06 05 04 03

Globe
Fearon

Pearson Learning Group

1-800-321-3106
www.pearsonlearning.com

CONTENTS

ABOUT THE AUTHOR

Charlotte Brontë was born in northern England in 1816. Her father was a clergyman and Charlotte spent most of her life in rural areas. Charlotte's mother died when Charlotte was only four. After her death, Charlotte and her brother and four sisters were left pretty much on their own.

Charlotte went to boarding school, taught, and worked as a governess for a time. With her sister Emily she went abroad to study French and German.

Jane Eyre is based on Charlotte's own experiences in the north of England and as a governess. The characters in the book are very different from those in novels written by other women of her time. This is one of the reasons that *Jane Eyre* was such a success.

By 1849 all of her sisters and her brother had died. Charlotte was left to care for her father, who had become almost blind. But Charlotte continued to write. Among her other books are; *The Professor, Villette,* and *Shirley.*

After their long engagement, which was broken off by her father, Charlotte and the Reverend Arthur Bell Nicholls finally married. She died less than a year later, in 1855.

ADAPTER'S NOTE

In preparing this edition of *Jane Eyre,* Charlotte Brontë's main purpose has been kept in mind. Since the book was originally published, however, language has changed. We have modified or omitted some passages and some vocabulary. We have, however, kept as much of the original as possible.

PREFACE

"A bold and haughty gentleman seemed somehow in the power of one of the lowest of his employees. He was so much in her power that even when she lifted her hand against his life, he dared not openly charge her . . . ." And so Jane Eyre wonders what mysterious hold the woman has over their employer.

The story of *Jane Eyre* is set in England in the early 1800s. It is both a mystery story and a love story. It tells of the lives of the rich, who lived in huge mansions and employed many servants. Jane is a governess, or tutor, in one of these mansions. She is poor and plain among the rich and beautiful.

From her very arrival at Thornfield Hall, Jane senses a mystery. And the mystery deepens as she gets to know her strange, and attractive, employer. She lives through spine-tingling shreiks, phantom footsteps, and blood-curdling laughs in the dead of night. A fire is set by an unknown hand, and a murder is attempted. Exciting events follow one right after another. And as the mystery grows, so does Jane's love for her employer.

1

"Are you Miss Eyre?"

"Yes."

"There's a person here waiting for you."

I jumped up, took my muff and umbrella, and hastened out into the yard of the inn. A man was standing by the open door, and in the dark street I dimly saw a horse and carriage.

"Is this your luggage?" asked the man when he saw me. He pointed to my trunk in the yard.

"Yes," said I.

He lifted the trunk onto the carriage, and then I got in. Before he closed the door, I asked him how far it was to Thornfield Hall.

"It's a matter of six miles."

"How long shall we be before we get there?"

"About an hour and a half."

He fastened the door, climbed to his own seat outside, and we started off. Our progress was slow, and I had time to think. I was content to be so near the end of my journey at last. As I leaned back in the carriage, I took out and read once again the letter from my new employer.

Since the references which you provided have proved satisfactory, I am pleased to offer you the position as governess at Thornfield Hall. You will have but one pupil, a little girl under ten years of age. The salary is thirty pounds per year.

The letter was signed by a Mrs. Fairfax. "I suppose,"

thought I, "Mrs. Fairfax is not one who likes grand and splendid things. I should judge that from the plainness of the servant and carriage. But so much the better! I lived among fine people only once, and I was very miserable with them. I wonder if she lives alone except for this little girl. If that is so and if she is at all friendly, I shall surely be able to get along with her. I will do my best. How far are we on our road now, I wonder?"

The roads were thick with mud. The night was misty. My driver let his horse walk all the way, and the hour and a half extended to two hours. At last he turned in his seat and said, "You're not far from Thornfield now."

About ten minutes later the driver got down and opened a pair of gates. After passing through, we slowly climbed a driveway and came upon the long front of a house. Candlelight gleamed from one of the windows, but all the rest were dark. The carriage stopped at the front door, which was opened by a maid. I got out and went in.

"Will you walk this way, ma'am?" said the girl. I followed her across a square hall with high doors all around. She showed me into a room that was lit by both a fire and candles. At first I was dazzled by the light after the darkness to which my eyes had been accustomed for two hours. When I could see, however, a cozy and agreeable picture presented itself to my view.

The room was small and snug. A round table was placed by a cheerful fire. Beside it in a high, old-fashioned armchair sat the neatest little old lady in a black silk gown and snowy white apron. Mrs. Fairfax was exactly like what I had imagined her to be, except that she was gentler and less stately looking. She was occupied in knitting.

A better introduction to a new position could scarcely be expected. Even for a humble person like me it was not too grand or embarrassing. As I entered, the old lady got up and came forward to meet me.

"How do you do, my dear? I am afraid you have had a tiring ride. John drives so slowly. You must be cold. Come to the fire."

"You are Mrs. Fairfax, I suppose?" said I.

"Yes, you are right. Do sit down."

She led me to her own chair and then began to remove my shawl and untie my bonnet strings. I begged her not to give herself so much trouble.

"Oh, it is no trouble. Your own hands must be almost numb with cold. Leah, make a little hot drink and cut a sandwich or two. Here are the keys of the storeroom."

She produced from her pocket a bunch of keys and gave them to the servant.

"Now, then, draw nearer to the fire," she continued. "You've brought your luggage with you, haven't you, my dear?"

"Yes, ma'am."

"I'll see that it is carried into your room," she said, hurrying away busily.

"She treats me like a visitor," thought I. "I little imagined such a welcome. I expected only coldness and stiffness. This is not like what I have heard of the treatment of governesses, but I must not be joyful too soon."

She returned. With her own hands she cleared the knitting and a book or two from the table to make room for the tray which Leah now brought. Then she herself handed me the refreshments. I felt rather confused at receiving so much attention from my employer. However, as she did not seem to consider she was doing anything out of place, I thought it better to take it quietly.

"Shall I have the pleasure of seeing Miss Fairfax tonight?" I asked.

"What did you say, my dear? I am a little deaf," replied the good lady, turning her ear toward my mouth.

I repeated the question more distinctly.

"Miss Fairfax? Oh, you mean little Miss Varens! Varens is the name of your future pupil."

"Indeed! Isn't she your daughter?"

"No. I have no family."

I wanted to ask in what way little Miss Varens was connected with her, but I remembered it was not polite to ask too many questions. Besides, I was sure to hear in time.

"I am so glad you have come," she continued as she sat down opposite me. "It will be quite pleasant living here now with a companion. You know in wintertime it is dull to be alone. I say alone although I am not really alone. But though Leah is a nice girl, and John and his wife are very decent people, they are only servants and one can't talk with them on terms of equality. One must keep them at a distance, for fear of losing one's authority. Of course, it has been better since little Adele Varens came with her nurse. A child makes a house alive all at once. And now you are here; so I shall be quite gay."

My heart really warmed to the worthy lady as I heard her talk. I drew my chair a little nearer to her and expressed my sincere wish that she might find my company as agreeable as she expected.

"But I'll not keep you sitting up late tonight," she said. "It is on the stroke of twelve now, and you have been traveling all day. You must feel tired. If you have warmed you feet well, I'll show you to your room."

She took her candle, and I followed her from the room. First she went to see if the hall door was fastened. Having taken the key from the lock, she led the way upstairs. The long corridor, into which the bedroom doors opened, looked as if it belonged to a church rather than a house. The candle held by Mrs. Fairfax threw ghostly shadows on the floor. A chilling draft of air swept along the hall, but the shiver which ran down my spine was not entirely from the cold. That gloomy darkness frightened me.

As we reached the door of my room, I thought to myself, "If any spirits really did walk the earth, this would be the very place for them."

2

Before breakfast next morning I decided to explore my new surroundings. I went out into the long corridor outside my bedroom and down the slippery oak steps to the main hall. There I stopped to look at two large pictures on the wall. One painting was of a cruel-looking man in armor; the other was of a lady whose hair was powdered and arranged in an old-fashioned way. It was now the year 1830, and I said to myself that ladies' hair had not been worn in such a style for quite a long time. "Perhaps those people were former owners of this place," I thought.

Everything appeared very splendid to me, for I was not accustomed to anything so grand. I admired the beautiful bronze lamp hanging from the ceiling, and I stopped to rub my hand over the oak wood of the great clock in the corner.

Then I stepped outside to look at the building. The house was three stories high and of considerable size. It had a gray front with little towers here and there along the top. I was thinking what a great place it was for one lonely little person like Mrs. Fairfax to live in, when that lady herself appeared at the door.

"What! Out already?" said she. "I see you are an early riser." I went up to her, and was received with a kiss and shake of the hand.

"How do you like Thornfield?" she asked. I told her I liked it very much. My fears of the previous night had vanished, and I made no mention of them.

"Yes," she said, "it is a pretty place. But I fear it will

be getting out of order, unless Mr. Rochester should take it into his head to come and live here permanently, or at least visit it more often. Great houses and fine grounds require the presence of their owner."

"Mr. Rochester!" I exclaimed. "Who is he?"

"The owner of Thornfield," she responded quietly. "His full name is Edward Fairfax Rochester. Did you not know he is the owner?"

Of course I did not; I had never heard of him before.

"I thought," I continued, "Thornfield belonged to you."

"To me? Bless you, child. What an idea! To me? I am only the housekeeper—the manager. To be sure, I am distantly related to the Rochesters, or at least my husband was. The present Mr. Rochester's mother was a Fairfax, and second cousin to my husband, but I never take advantage of the connection. In fact it is nothing to me. I consider myself quite in the light of an ordinary housekeeper. My employer is always considerate, and I expect nothing more."

"And the little girl—my pupil?"

"Mr. Rochester is her guardian. He asked me to find a governess for her. He intends to have her brought up here, I believe. Here she comes with her nurse." Now I understood much. This kind little widow was no great lady, but an employee like myself. I did not like her the worse for that. On the contrary, I felt more pleased than ever. She and I were real equals. So much the better.

As I was thinking about this discovery, a little girl came running up the lawn. She was just a child, perhaps seven or eight years old, slightly built, with a pale, small-featured face, and thick hair falling in curls to her waist.

"Good morning, Miss Adele," said Mrs. Fairfax. "Come and speak to the lady who is to teach you, and to make you a clever woman some day."

"Is that my governess?" she asked in French, pointing to me.

"Indeed it is," replied the nurse in the same language.

"Are they foreigners?" I inquired in amazement.

"Yes," Mrs. Fairfax told me. "Adele was born in France and never left it till six months ago. When she first came here, she could speak no English. Now she can speak it a little. I don't understand her because she mixes her English so with French, but you will make out her meaning very well, I suppose."

Fortunately I had had the advantage of being taught French by a French lady. I was not likely to have any difficulty in understanding Mademoiselle Adele. She came and shook hands with me when she heard that I was her governess. As I led her in to breakfast, I addressed some remarks to her in her own language. She replied briefly at first. However, after we were seated at the table and she had examined me for ten minutes with her large hazel eyes, she suddenly began chattering rapidly.

"Ah," cried she in French, "you speak my language as well as Mr. Rochester does. I can talk to you as I can to him, and so can Sophie. She will be glad. Nobody here understands her. Madame Fairfax is all English. Sophie is my nurse. She came with me over the sea in a great ship with a chimney that smoked—how it did smoke! —and I was sick, and so was Sophie, and so was Mr. Rochester. Mr. Rochester lay down on a sofa in a pretty room called the salon, and Sophie and I had little beds in another place. I nearly fell out of mine; it was like a shelf. And, Mademoiselle—what is your name?"

"Eyre—Jane Eyre."

"Aire? Bah! I cannot say it. Well, our ship stopped at a great city in the morning before it was quite daylight. It was a huge city with very dark houses and all smoky; not at all like the pretty, clean town I came from. Mr. Rochester carried me in his arms over a plank to the land, and Sophie came after. We all got into a coach, which took us to a beautiful large house, larger than this and finer, called a hotel. We stayed there nearly a week. Sophie and I used to walk every day in a great green place full of trees, called the Park; and there were many children there besides me, and a pond with beautiful birds in it, that I fed with crumbs."

"Can you understand her when she runs on so fast?" asked Mrs. Fairfax.

I understood her very well, for I had been accustomed to the quick tongue of my former French teacher.

"I wish," continued the good lady, "you would ask her a question or two about her parents. I wonder if she remembers them."

"Adele," I inquired, "with whom did you live when you were in that pretty, clean town you spoke of?"

"I lived long ago with Mama, but she is gone to the Heavenly Kingdom. Mama used to teach me to dance and sing, and to say verses. A great many gentlemen and ladies came to see Mama, and I used to dance before them, or sit on their knees and sing to them. I liked it. Shall I let you hear me sing now?"

"No, not now. But after your mama went to the Heavenly Kingdom, as you say, with whom did you live then?"

"With Madame Frederic and her husband. She took care of me, but she is not related to me. I think she is poor, for she had not so fine a house as Mama. I was not there long. Mr. Rochester asked me if I would like to go and live with him in England, and I said yes; for I knew Mr. Rochester before I knew Madame Frederic. He was always kind to me and gave me pretty dresses and toys. But you see he has not kept his word, for he has brought me to England, and now he has gone back himself, and I never see him."

After breakfast, Adele and I went off to the library, which was to be used as the schoolroom. I found my pupil sufficiently willing, though she was not used to regular study of any kind. I felt it would not be wise to demand too much of her at first. At noontime, after I had talked to her a great deal and had got her to learn a little, I allowed her to return to her nurse. I then proposed to spend the time before dinner in drawing some little sketches for her use.

As I was going upstairs to fetch my portfolio and pencils, Mrs. Fairfax called to me. "Your morning school hours are over now, I suppose," she said. The doors of the room she was in stood open. It was a large room with purple chairs and curtains, a Turkish carpet, one great window of stained glass, and a high ceiling. Mrs. Fairfax was dusting some vases which stood on a sideboard.

"What a beautiful room!" I exclaimed as I looked around. I had never before seen anything so splendid.

"Yes. This is the dining room. I have just opened the window to let in a little air and sunshine. Everything gets so damp in places that are seldom used."

"In what order you keep these rooms, Mrs. Fairfax!" said I. "No dust, no canvas coverings! Except that the air feels chilly, one would think they were used every day."

"Why, Miss Eyre, although Mr. Rochester's visits here are few, they are always sudden and unexpected.

As I noticed that it annoyed him to have things put in order on his arrival, I thought it best to keep the rooms always ready."

"Is Mr. Rochester difficult to please?"

"Not particularly so. But he has a gentleman's tastes and habits, and he expects to have things managed to suit them."

"Do you like him? Is he generally liked?"

"Oh, yes! The family has always been respected here. Almost all the land in this neighborhood, as far as you can see, has belonged to the Rochesters for the longest time."

"Well, but leaving the subject of his land aside, do you like him? Is he liked for himself?"

"I have no cause to do otherwise than like him. I believe he is considered a just and liberal landlord by his tenants, but he has never lived much among them."

"But has he no peculiarities? What sort of person is he?"

"Oh! He is rather peculiar, perhaps. He has traveled a great deal, and seen a great deal of the world, I should think. I dare say he is clever, but I never had much conversation with him."

"In what way is he peculiar?"

"I don't know—it is not easy to describe—nothing striking, but you feel it when he speaks to you. You cannot always be sure whether he is in jest or earnest, whether he is pleased or the contrary. You don't thoroughly understand him, in short—at least, I don't. But it is of no consequence, for he is a very good master."

When we left the dining room, she proposed to show me the rest of the house. I followed her upstairs and downstairs, admiring as I went, for all was well-arranged and handsome. While we were passing through the third story, I inquired, "Do the servants sleep in these rooms?" I nodded toward the bedroom doors nearby.

"No, they occupy smaller ones to the back. No one ever sleeps here. One would almost say that, if there were a ghost at Thornfield Hall, it would haunt this part of the house."

"So I think. Have you no ghost at Thornfield, then?"

"None that I ever heard of," replied Mrs. Fairfax, smiling.

"Nor any legends or ghost stories?"

"I believe not. And yet it is said the Rochesters were a wild and violent people in the old days. Perhaps, though, that is the reason they rest quietly in their graves now."

"Where are we going next?" I asked, for she was moving away.

"Up to the roof. Will you come and see the view from there?"

I followed her up a very narrow staircase to the attic, and from there by a ladder and through a trap door to the roof of the Hall. I was now on a level with the nests of crows in the nearby trees. Leaning over and looking far down, I gazed at the grounds, which were laid out before me like a map. No feature in the scene was unusual, but all was pleasing. When I turned from it and again passed the trap door, I could scarcely see my way down the ladder. The attic seemed black as a tomb compared with that sunlit scene over which I had been gazing with delight.

Mrs. Fairfax stayed behind for a moment to fasten the trap door. By groping, I found the exit from the attic and proceeded to go down the narrow staircase into the long hall of the third story. This hall was narrow, low, and dim, with only one little window at the far end. Indeed, it was so dim that Mrs. Fairfax had left a lighted candle beside the staircase. With its two rows of small black doors all shut, the hall looked like a corridor in Bluebeard's castle.

While I paced softly on, the last sound I expected to hear in so quiet a place struck my ear. It was a curious laugh without any real amusement in it. I stopped. The sound stopped too, but only for an instant. At first it had been very low, though distinct. When it began again, it was louder. It finished in a shrill sound that woke an echo in every lonely room, though it came from but one, and I could have pointed out its door.

"Mrs. Fairfax!" I called out, for I now heard her coming down the great stairs. "Did you hear that loud laugh? Who is it?"

"Some of the servants, very likely," she answered. "Perhaps Grace Poole." She picked up the candle so as to light the way.

"Did you hear it?" I again inquired.

"Yes, plainly. I often hear her. She sews in one of these rooms. Sometimes Leah is with her. They are frequently noisy together."

The laugh was repeated in its low tone, and ended in an odd murmur.

"Grace!" exclaimed Mrs. Fairfax.

I really did not expect any Grace to answer, for the laugh was like none that I had ever heard. If the time had not been midday and without any condition of ghostliness attached to it, I should have been superstitiously afraid.

The door nearest me opened, and a servant came out. She was a woman of between thirty and forty, a square-made figure, red-haired, and with a hard, plain face.

"Too much noise, Grace," said Mrs. Fairfax. "Remember directions!" Grace nodded silently and went in.

"She is a person who sews and assists Leah in her housemaid's work," continued the widow, "not altogether suitable in some points, but she does well enough."

I did not question Mrs. Fairfax's statement, but I could not help wondering a little. That was the beginning of the puzzle of Grace Poole.

3

In the following days, I frequently heard Grace Poole's laugh: the same shrillness, the same low, slow ha! ha! I heard, too, her queer murmurs, stranger than her laugh. There were days when she was quite silent, but there were others when I could not account for the sounds she made. Sometimes I saw her. She would come out of her room with a basin or a plate or an empty tray in her hand. Down she would go to the kitchen and shortly return, generally bearing a full tray covered with a cloth. I made some attempts to draw her into conversation, but she seemed a person of few words. A brief reply usually cut short every effort of that sort.

The other members of the household, John and his wife, Leah, the housemaid, and Sophie, the French nurse, were decent people, but in no respect remarkable. With Sophie I used to speak French, and sometimes I asked her questions about her native country, but she was rather dull. At that time there was no one at Thornfield to give it spirit or relieve the dullness of our daily routine, but that was soon to be changed.

October, November, December passed away. One afternoon in January, Mrs. Fairfax had begged a holiday for Adele from her lessons because she had a cold. It was a fine, calm day, though very cool. I was tired of sitting still in the library through a whole long morning. Mrs. Fairfax had just written a letter which was waiting to be mailed; so I put on my bonnet and cloak and volunteered to carry it to Hay. The distance, two miles, would be a pleasant winter afternoon walk.

The air was fresh and clear. Enjoying my errand, I did not hasten. The afternoon wore away, and evening came while I was yet a distance from Thornfield. My road lay across a hilltop above which sat the rising moon.

As I walked, I became aware of a noise behind me, sounding faint at first, then louder and louder. A positive tramp, tramp! A metallic clatter!

The din was on the roadway. A horse was coming; the windings of the lane yet hid it, but it approached. In those days I was young, and all sorts of fancies bright and dark occupied my mind. The memories of nursery stories were there among others. As this horse approached, I watched for it to appear through the dusk. I remembered certain tales about a spirit called a "Gytrash," which in the form of horse, mule, or large dog haunted lonely ways and sometimes came upon late travelers, as this horse was now coming upon me.

It was very near, but not yet in sight. Then, in addition to the tramp, tramp, I heard a rush under the hedge, and close by glided a great dog, whose black and white color made him a distinct object against the trees. It was exactly like a Gytrash in a story—a lionlike creature with long hair and a huge head. It passed me quietly enough, however, not staying to look up in my face as I half expected it would. The horse followed—a tall steed, and on its back a rider. The man, the human being, broke the spell at once. Nothing ever rode the Gytrash. It was always alone. No Gytrash was this—only a traveler taking the shortcut to Millcote. He passed, and I went on a few steps. Suddenly there was a sliding sound and an exclamation of "What the deuce is up now?" A clattering tumble arrested my attention. Man and horse were down; they had slipped on the sheet of ice which glazed the roadway. The dog came bounding back, and seeing his master in difficulties and hearing the hoarse groan, barked till the evening hills echoed the sound. He sniffed around the fallen group, and then he ran up to me. It was all he could do. There was no other help at hand to summon. I obeyed him and walked down to the traveler, who was by this time struggling free of his steed. His efforts were so vigorous, I thought he could not be much hurt. But I asked him, "Can I do anything?"

"You must just stand on one side," he answered as he rose. I did. Then, by much pulling and pushing he got the horse back upon its feet. The traveler now felt his own leg to see whether it was in good condition. Evidently something was wrong, for he limped to a nearby tree stump and sat down.

I was in the mood for being useful; I now drew near him again.

"If you are hurt, and want help, sir, I can fetch someone either from Thornfield Hall or from Hay."

"Thank you. I shall be all right. I have no broken bones—only a sprain." Again he stood up and tried his foot, but the result brought forth a groan.

The moon was bright; I could see him plainly. His figure was enveloped in a riding cloak, fur-collared and fastened with steel clasps. I noted that he was of medium height and considerable width of chest. He had a dark face with stern features. His eyes looked full of anger just now. He was about thirty-five. I felt no fear of him, and but little shyness.

"I cannot think of leaving you, sir, at so late an hour in this lonely lane, till I see that you are fit to mount your horse."

He looked at me when I said this. He had hardly turned his eyes in my direction before.

"I should think you ought to be at home yourself," said he, "if you have a home in this neighborhood. Where do you come from?"

"From just below; and I am not at all afraid of being out late when there is moonlight."

"You live just below. Do you mean at that house with the towers?" He pointed to Thornfield Hall, on which the moon cast a gleam, bringing it out distinct and pale from the woods.

"Yes, sir."

"Whose house is it?"

"Mr. Rochester's."

"Do you know Mr. Rochester?"

"No, I have never seen him."

"He is not living there, then?"

"No."

"Can you tell me where he is?"

"I cannot."

"You are not a servant at the hall, of course. You are—" He stopped, ran his eye over my dress, which, as usual, was quite simple. He seemed puzzled to decide what I was. I helped him.

"I am the governess."

"Ah, the governess!" he repeated. "Deuce take me, if I had not forgotten! The governess!" In two minutes he rose from the stump. His face expressed pain when he tried to move.

"I cannot ask you to fetch help," he said, "but you may help me a little yourself, if you will be so kind."

"Yes, sir."

"You have not an umbrella that I can use as a cane?" he asked.

"No."

"Try to get hold of my horse's bridle and lead him to me. You are not afraid, are you?"

I should have been afraid to touch a horse when alone, but when told to do it, I obeyed. I put down my muff on the stump and went up to the tall steed. I tried to catch the bridle, but the horse was spirited, and would not let me come near its head. I made effort after effort, though in vain. Meantime, I was greatly afraid of its trampling forefeet. The traveler waited and watched for some time, and at last he laughed.

"I see," he said, "that you will never make a successful trainer of horses. I must beg you to come here."

I came. "Excuse me," he continued. "Necessity compels me to make you useful."

He laid a heavy hand on my shoulder, and leaning on me, limped to his horse. Having once caught the bridle, he mastered the animal immediately and sprang to his saddle. His face twisted grimly as he made the effort, for it made his sprain worse.

"Now," said he, releasing his lower lip from a hard bite, "just hand me my whip. It lies there under the hedge."

I searched and found it.

"Thank you," he said, as he took it from my hand.

A touch of his spur made his horse bound away. The dog followed swiftly behind. All three vanished.

I did not like coming back to Thornfield. To pass its threshold was to return to dullness. I would not enjoy crossing the silent hall, climbing the dark staircase, sitting in my own lonely little room, and then meeting quiet Mrs. Fairfax and spending the long winter evening with her. It would spoil the little feeling of excitement awakened by my walk.

The hall was not dark, nor yet was it well-lit by the high bronze lamp. However, a warm glow came from the great dining room, whose door stood open and showed a cheerful fire in the grate. Its light revealed a group of people near the mantelpiece. I had scarcely glanced in when the door closed.

I hastened to Mrs. Fairfax's room. A fire was there too, but no candle, and no Mrs. Fairfax. Instead, all alone, sitting upright on the rug and gazing at the blaze, was a great black and white long-haired dog, just like the Gytrash of the lane.

I caressed him, and he wagged his great tail, but he seemed a weird creature to be alone with, and I could not tell from where he had come. I rang the bell, for I wanted a candle. I wanted, too, to get an account of this visitor. Leah entered.

"What dog is this?"

"He came with master."

"With whom?"

"With master—Mr. Rochester—he has just arrived."

"Indeed! And is Mrs. Fairfax with him?"

"Yes, and Miss Adele. They are in the dining room. John has gone for the doctor, for master has had an accident. His horse fell and his ankle is sprained."

"Did the horse fall in Hay Lane?"

"Yes. Coming downhill, it slipped on some ice."

"Ah! Bring me a candle, will you, Leah?"

Leah brought it. She entered, followed by Mrs. Fairfax, who repeated the news. She added that Mr. Carter, the doctor, had come, and was now with Mr. Rochester. Then she hurried out to give orders about tea, and I went upstairs to take off my things.

Matters now became different. Adele and I next day had to vacate the library. It would be in daily use as a reception room for callers. A fire was lit in a room upstairs, and I carried our books there and arranged it for the future schoolroom. I noticed in the course of the morning that Thornfield Hall was a changed place. No longer silent as a church, it echoed every hour or two to a knock at the door, or a clang of the bell. Steps, too, often sounded in the hall, and new voices spoke in different keys below. For my part, I liked it better.

Toward twilight, Mrs. Fairfax entered my room. "Mr. Rochester would be glad if you and your pupil would take tea with him in the drawing room this evening," said she. "He has been so much engaged all day that he could not ask to see you before."

"When is his teatime?" I inquired.

"Oh, at six o'clock. He keeps early hours in the country. You had better change your dress now. I will go with you and fasten it. Here is a candle."

"Is it necessary to change?"

"Yes, you had better. I always dress for the evening when Mr. Rochester is here."

When we came into the drawing room, two wax candles stood lighted on the table, and two on the mantelpiece. Basking in the light and heat of a superb fire lay the dog, Pilot. Adele knelt near him. Sitting in a chair appeared Mr. Rochester, his foot supported by a cushion. He was looking at Adele and the dog. The fire shone full on his face. I knew my traveler with his broad, black eyebrows, his square forehead, and his black hair. I recognized his stern mouth, chin, and jaw—yes, all three were very stern, and no mistake. His was a good figure in the athletic sense—broad-chested and without too much weight, tall, but not too graceful.

Mr. Rochester must have been aware of the entrance of Mrs. Fairfax and myself, but it appeared he was not in the mood to notice us, for he never lifted his head as we approached.

"Here is Miss Eyre, sir," said Mrs. Fairfax in her quiet way. He bowed, still not taking his eyes from the dog and child.

"Let Miss Eyre be seated," said he. There was something in his impatient tone which seemed to express without saying it, "What the deuce is it to me whether Miss Eyre is there or not? At this moment I do not intend to speak to her."

I sat down without embarrassment. A polite reception would probably have confused me. It might have made me shy. This cold lack of interest only amused me.

Mrs. Fairfax seemed to think it necessary that someone should be friendly, and she began to talk.

"Madam, I should like some tea," was the only reply she got from Mr. Rochester. She hastened to ring the bell. When the tray came, she proceeded to arrange the cups, saucers, and spoons in a great hurry. Adele and I went to the table, but the master did not leave his chair.

"Will you hand Mr. Rochester his cup?" said Mrs. Fairfax to me. "Adele might perhaps spill it."

I did as requested, and he took the cup from my hand. Adele, thinking this a favorable moment to make a request for me, cried out, "Monsieur, didn't you bring a gift for Mademoiselle Eyre?"

"Who talks of gifts?" said he gruffly. "Did you expect a present, Miss Eyre? Are you fond of presents?"

He searched my face with his dark and piercing eyes.

"I hardly know, sir. I have little experience of them. They are generally thought pleasant things."

"Generally thought? But what do *you* think?"

"One should consider what the present is and why it is given, before saying what one thinks of it."

"Miss Eyre, you are not so simple as Adele. She demands a present noisily the moment she sees me. You beat about the bush."

"Because I have no reason to receive gifts. Adele has the claim of old acquaintance, and she says you have always been in the habit of giving her playthings; but I am a stranger, and have done nothing to entitle me to a present."

"Oh, don't fall back on modesty! I have examined Adele, and find you have taken great pains with her. She is not bright. She has no talents; yet in a short time she has made much improvement."

"Sir, you have now given me my present. I am obliged to you. It is what teachers most desire: praise of their pupils' progress."

"Humph!" said Mr. Rochester, and he took his tea in silence.

"Come to the fire," said the master when the tray was taken away. Mrs. Fairfax had settled into a corner with her knitting, while Adele was leading me by the hand around the room, showing me the beautiful books and ornaments. I obeyed, as it was my duty. Adele wanted to take a seat on my knee, but she was ordered to amuse herself with Pilot.

"You have been in my house three months?"

"Yes, sir."

"And you came from—?"

"From Lowood school, in Westshire."

"Ah! a charity school. How long were you there?"

"Eight years."

"Eight years! You must hold fast to life. I thought half the time in such a place would have worn out any-one! No wonder you have the look of being from another world. When you came upon me in Hay Lane last night, I thought of fairy tales and had half a mind to demand whether you had bewitched my horse. I am not sure yet. Who are your parents?"

"I have none."

"Do you remember them?"

"No."

"I thought not. Fairies really have no parents. And so you were waiting for your people when I passed you on the road?"

"For whom, sir?"

"For your people—the fairies. It was just the proper moonlight evening for them. Did I break through one of your magic rings to cause you to spread that ice on the roadway?"

I shook my head. "The fairies all went out of England a hundred years ago," said I, speaking as seriously as he had done. "And not even in Hay Lane, or the fields about it, could you find a trace of them. I don't think the moon will ever shine on their dances again."

Mrs. Fairfax had dropped her knitting. With raised eyebrows she seemed to be wondering what sort of talk this was.

"Well," continued Mr. Rochester, "if you have no parents, you must have some sort of relatives. Have you any uncles and aunts?"

"Only an uncle who lives in a distant place. He is on the island of Madeira."

"And your home?"

"I have none."

"Where do your brothers and sisters live?"

"I have no brothers or sisters."

"How did you happen to come here?"

"I advertised, and Mrs. Fairfax answered my advertisement."

"Yes," said the good lady, "and I am thankful for the choice I made. Miss Eyre has been a valuable companion to me, and a kind and careful teacher to Adele."

"Don't trouble yourself to tell me how worthy she is," returned Mr. Rochester. "I shall judge for myself. Miss Eyre, have you ever lived in a town?"

"No, sir."

"Have you known many people?"

"None but the pupils and teachers of Lowood."

"Have you read much?"

"Only such books as I could get, which were not many."

"You have lived the life of a nun. No doubt you are well drilled in religion. I understand that the man who directs Lowood is a parson, is he not?"

"Yes, sir."

"What age were you when you went to Lowood?"

"About ten."

"And you stayed there eight years. Then you are now eighteen, aren't you?"

I agreed.

"Arithmetic, you see, is useful. Without its aid I should hardly have been able to guess how old you are. Your appearance is older than your actual age. Now what did you learn at Lowood? Can you play the piano?"

"A little."

"Of course. That is the usual answer. Go into the library—I mean, if you please. Excuse my tone of command. I am used to saying 'Do this,' and it is done. I cannot change my customary habits for one new person. Go, then, into the library. Take a candle with you. Leave the door open. Sit down to the piano, and play a tune."

I departed, obeying his directions.

"Enough!" he called out in a few minutes. "You play *a little*, I see, just like any other English schoolgirl. Perhaps you play better than some girls."

I closed the piano, and returned. Mr. Rochester continued, "Adele showed me some sketches this morning, which she said were yours. I don't know whether they were entirely of your doing. Probably someone helped you. Isn't that so?"

"No, indeed!" I declared.

"Ah! That hurts your pride. Well, fetch me your portfolio if you are sure its contents are original, but don't try to deceive me. I can recognize a copied drawing or one with which a beginner has been helped by a teacher."

"Then I will say nothing, and you shall judge for yourself, sir."

I brought the portfolio from the library.

"Fetch the table," said he, and I wheeled it to his chair. Adele and Mrs. Fairfax drew near to see the pictures.

"No crowding," said Mr. Rochester. "Take the drawings from my hand as I finish with them, but don't push your faces up to mine."

He carefully studied each sketch and painting. Three he laid aside; the others he swept away from him.

"Take them off to the other table, Mrs. Fairfax," said he, "and look at them with Adele. Miss Eyre, take your seat, and answer my questions. I see that these pictures were done by one person. Was that person you?"

"Yes."

"And when did you find time to do them? They have taken much time and some thought."

"I did them in the last two vacations I spent at Lowood, when I had no other work to do."

"Where did you find the scenes to draw?"

"In my head."

"That head I see now on your shoulders?"

"Yes, sir."

"Has it other things of the same kind inside it?"

"I should think it may have. I should hope it has even better things."

He spread the pictures before him and again studied them.

"Yes, you have a little of the artist's skill and science," he said finally. "There—put the drawings away!"

I had scarcely tied the strings of the portfolio when he said abruptly, "It is nine o'clock. What are you doing, Miss Eyre, to let Adele sit up so long? Take her to bed. I wish you all good night now."

He motioned towards the door, to show that he was tired of our company and wished to dismiss us. Mrs. Fairfax folded up her knitting. I took my portfolio. We curtseyed to him, received a cold bow in return, and so went out.

"You said Mr. Rochester was not peculiar, Mrs. Fairfax," I remarked when I joined her in her room after putting Adele to bed.

"Well, is he?"

"I think so. He is very changeful and abrupt."

"True. No doubt he may appear so to a stranger, but I am so accustomed to his manner, I never think of it. Then if he has peculiar ways, allowance should be made."

"Why?"

"Partly we should forgive him because it is his nature—and we can none of us help our nature. Partly we should make allowances for him because he has painful thoughts to make his spirits uneasy."

"What about?"

"Family troubles, for one thing."

"But he has no family."

"Not now, but he has had—or, at least, relatives. He lost his elder brother, Rowland, a few years ago."

"His *elder* brother?"

"Yes. The present Mr. Edward Rochester has not been very long in possession of the property, only about nine years."

"Nine years is long enough. Was he so very fond of his brother as to be still mourning his loss?"

"Why, no—perhaps not. I believe there were some misunderstandings between them. Mr. Rowland Rochester was not quite just to Mr. Edward, and perhaps he influenced his father against him. The old gentleman was fond of money and anxious to keep the family fortune together. He made a will leaving the entire property to the elder son, Rowland, because he did not want to divide the large estate into two smaller parts. Yet the father was anxious that Mr. Edward should have wealth, too. Old Mr. Rochester and Mr. Rowland arranged to bring Mr. Edward into a fortune, but there was dirty work done to bring it about. Just what it was I never clearly knew, but Mr. Edward's spirit could not bear what he had to suffer in it. He is not very forgiving.

He broke with his family, and now for many years he has led an unsettled kind of life. I don't think he has ever been at Thornfield for two weeks together, since the death of his brother left him master of the estate. Then perhaps he has still other reasons for avoiding the old place."

"Why should he avoid it?"

"I have sometimes thought I knew, but there is still some mystery to it which has not yet been cleared up in my own mind. Therefore I had rather say nothing about it."

I should have liked her to say something clearer, but it was evident, indeed, that she wished me to drop the subject, which I did accordingly.

5

For several days afterward I saw little of Mr. Rochester. In the mornings he seemed much engaged with business. In the afternoons, gentlemen from the nearby town of Millcote called and sometimes stayed to dine with him. When his sprain was well enough to permit horse exercise, he rode a good deal. He generally did not come back till late at night.

During this time even Adele was seldom asked to come to him. All my acquaintance with him was limited to an occasional meeting in the hall or on the stairs. Then he would sometimes pass me haughtily and coldly, just giving me a distant nod or a cool glance, and sometimes he would bow and smile with gentlemanlike friendliness. His changes of mood did not offend me, because I saw that I had nothing to do with them. Their rise and fall depended on causes quite unconnected with me.

One day he had company to dinner and sent for my portfolio of sketches in order to show its contents to his friends. The gentlemen went away early to attend a public meeting at Millcote, as Mrs. Fairfax informed me. The night being wet, Mr. Rochester did not go with them. Soon after they were gone, he rang the bell. A message came that Adele and I were to go downstairs. I brushed Adele's hair and made her neat. I made certain that I was myself in my usual order. We went down, Adele wondering whether the box of gifts promised by Mr. Rochester had at last come. Owing to some mistake, its arrival had been delayed. She was pleased. There it stood on the table when we entered the dining room. She appeared to know it by instinct.

"My presents! My presents!" exclaimed she, running towards it.

"Yes—there is your box at last. Take it into a corner and amuse yourself with operating upon it," said the voice of Mr. Rochester, coming from deep down in an immense easy chair at the fireside. "And mind," he continued, "don't bother me with any details of the process and don't tell me about the condition of the insides. Let your operation be done in silence; do you understand, child?"

Adele seemed scarcely to need the warning. She had already retired to a sofa with her treasure, and was busy untying the cord which fastened the lid. Having removed this, and having lifted certain silvery envelopes of tissue paper, she merely exclaimed: "Oh goodness! How pretty!" Then she remained absorbed in overjoyed inspection of these wonders.

"Is Miss Eyre there?" now demanded the master, half rising from his seat to look around to the door, near which I still stood.

"Ah! well. Come forward. Be seated here." He drew a chair near his own. "I am not fond of the chatter of children," he continued, "for, old bachelor as I am, I have no pleasant feelings connected with listening to them. It would be unbearable for me to pass a whole evening conversing with a brat. Don't draw that chair further off, Miss Eyre. Sit down exactly where I placed it—if you please, that is. Confound these politenesses! I continually forget them. Nor do I particularly care for simple-minded old ladies. By-the-by, I must keep my old housekeeper in mind. It won't do to neglect her.

She is a Fairfax or at least was wed to one, and blood is said to be thicker than water."

He rang and sent an invitation to Mrs. Fairfax, who soon arrived, knitting-basket in hand.

"Good evening, madam. I sent for you to perform a good deed. I have forbidden Adele to talk to me about her presents, and she is bursting to discuss them. Have the goodness to serve her as a listener. It will be one of the kindest acts you ever performed."

Adele, indeed, no sooner saw Mrs. Fairfax than she called her to her sofa and there quickly filled her lap with the porcelain, the ivory, the waxen contents of her treasure chest.

"Now that I have performed the part of a good host," continued Mr. Rochester, "by helping my guests amuse each other, I ought to attend to my own pleasure. Miss Eyre, draw your chair still a little further forward. You are yet too far back. I cannot see without disturbing my position in this comfortable chair, which I have no intention of doing."

I did as I was bidden though I would much rather have remained somewhat in the shadow, but Mr. Rochester had such a direct way of giving orders, it seemed a matter of course to obey him promptly.

We were, as I have said, in the dining room. The lamp, which had been lit for dinner, filled the room with a rich glow of light. The large fire was all red and clear. The purple curtains hung full and soft before the lofty window. Everything was still, except the quiet chatter of Adele and the beat of winter rain against the panes.

Mr. Rochester looked different from what I had seen him look before. He was not quite so stern—much less gloomy. There was a smile on his lips. His eyes sparkled, and I thought that he had probably drunk a glass or two of wine.

He had been looking for two minutes at the fire, and I had been looking the same length of time at him when, turning suddenly, he caught my gaze fastened on his face.

"You examine me, Miss Eyre," said he. "Do you think me handsome?"

The answer somehow slipped from my tongue before I was aware: "No, sir."

"Ah! By my word! There is something odd about you," said he. "You have the air of a quiet little nothing, as you sit with your hands before you, and your eyes generally bent on the carpet. But when one asks you a question or makes a remark to which you are obliged to reply, you rap out as sharp a statement as a lawyer defending his client in a court. What do you mean by it?"

"Sir, I was too plain. I beg your pardon. I ought to have replied that it was not easy to give an answer to a question about appearances. I should have said that tastes differ or that beauty is of little importance, or something of that sort."

"You ought to have replied no such thing. Beauty of little importance, indeed! Go on! What fault do you find with me, pray? I suppose I have all my limbs and all my features like any other man?"

"Mr. Rochester, allow me to take back my first answer. I intended no offense. It was only a blunder."

"Just so. I think so. And you shall answer for it. Can you read character in a face? Read mine."

I gazed straight at him for a full minute, and he stared back without blinking. His forehead was high, which some say is a sign of great intelligence. But his features were stern and showed little kindliness.

"Now, ma'am, am I a fool?"

"Far from it, sir. You would perhaps think me rude if I inquired in return whether you are a soft-hearted and charitable man?"

"No, young lady, I am not a soft-hearted man, but neither am I an exceptionally hard-hearted one. What is more, I have a conscience. I would not willingly hurt anyone. Nor would I neglect a responsibility or fail to repay a debt."

He leaned toward me and spoke in a lower tone so that the child and Mrs. Fairfax might not hear. "Adele, for instance, is a responsibility that I have accepted. She is the daughter of a French lady who once did me a good turn. To pay off the debt, I have taken this child to bring up."

"That was a good deed, sir—one which I certainly approve of. If I am to be honest, however, I must say that it does not require a very warm heart to perform such an act. An honorable man would pay his debts, however great the cost or difficulty. It takes a man of real feeling to do a kindness for its own sake, when no debt is involved."

"Well spoken," declared Mr. Rochester. "You speak like a lawyer, and you take a man's measure better than a tailor. But let me tell you that I once had a more tender heart. When I was as old as you, I was a soft-hearted fellow enough. I was always ready to help those weaker, more ignorant, or unluckier than myself. But fortune has knocked me about since, and now I am as hard and tough as an India-rubber ball."

With this he rose from his chair and stood, leaning his arm on the marble mantelpiece. I am sure most people would have thought him ugly if they had con-

sidered only his general appearance. Yet there was some power about him which made him attractive—especially to me. I was to learn later that he was liked by all.

"I wanted to speak to some friendly person tonight," he remarked, "and that is why I sent for you. Talk to me now. It will clear my mind of black thoughts which eat into my spirit like a disease eating into flesh."

"I am willing to amuse you if I can, sir, but I do not know what will interest you. Ask me questions, and I will do my best to answer them."

"Well, then," he said. "Here is a question. Do you mind if sometimes I treat you as if you were another man—a good friend? Do you mind if I deal with you without all the politeness and fuss that a gentleman is supposed to use with a lady?"

I smiled. I thought to myself that Mr. Rochester seemed to forget he was paying me thirty pounds a year to serve him.

Noticing my expression, he said, "That smile is very good, but speak, too."

"I was thinking, sir, that very few masters would bother to ask whether their paid employees were hurt by their treatment."

"Paid employees! What, you are my paid employee, are you? Oh, yes, I had almost forgotten that. But in our conversation I should like you to forget that I am your employer. I should like to hear your honest opinion and not have you always agreeing with me simply because I pay you a salary."

"I am sure, sir, that no free-born person would give up the right to speak an honest opinion, even for a salary."

"Nonsense!" he cried. "Most people will do anything for a salary. However, I like your spirit. Not three in three thousand young girls, just out of school, would have answered me as you have done. But perhaps I am judging you too soon. You may be no better than the rest. You may have bad faults to balance your few good ones."

"And so may you," I thought to myself. Although I said nothing aloud, he seemed to read the idea in my mind.

"I know what you are thinking," said he. "Yes, I have plenty of faults of my own. I know it, and I don't try to excuse them. I certainly cannot afford to be too hard on others. I have led a sinful life, for which I may well be blamed. However, I like to think that the fault is not entirely my own, and that it has been partly due to ill fortune. I was started on the wrong track at the age of twenty-one, and I have never got back to the right way since. But I might have been very different. I might have been as good as you. I envy your clean conscience and peace of mind. Do you wonder that I confess this to you? I believe that often during your life people will tell you their secrets. That is because you listen without scorning their mistakes, but with a kind of sympathy which is part of your nature."

"How can you tell that, sir?" I asked.

"I can tell it easily," he replied. "Therefore I can talk to you almost as freely as if I were writing my thoughts in a diary. I suppose you would say that I should have fought against the ill fortune which dragged me down into a sinful life. So I should, but you see I did not. I wish I had—God knows I do! I regret it. Fear regret when you are tempted into evil, Miss Eyre. Regret is the poison of life."

"Is there no cure for that poison, sir?"

"Reform may be its cure. I could reform, but what

is the use? Since true happiness is impossible for me, I have a right to get some pleasure out of life—even if it is sinful pleasures."

"To speak the truth, sir, I cannot agree with you. You said that you were not as good as you should like to be, and that you regretted it. It seems to me that if you tried hard, you would find it possible to become a man whom you yourself would respect. If from this day you began to correct your thoughts and actions, you would in a few years become such a person as might be respected and admired by all—including yourself."

"Rightly said, Miss Eyre. You have convinced me. At this moment I am full of good intentions."

"Sir?"

"I am making new rules for my conduct," said Mr. Rochester, "and I am determined they shall last. Certainly my friends and my deeds shall be different from what they have been."

"And better?" I asked.

"Yes, better—so much as pure gold is better than lead."

At a later time Mr. Rochester opened for me other pages in the book of his life. It was a dark tale of a rich young man wasting himself in worthless pleasures. He had spent much of his time in Europe, traveling far and wide, and living for short periods in one city or another. Those whom he had had as companions, both men and women, were not of high character, nor were their ways of living good. From what he told me, I learned that Mr. Rochester had indeed lived a wicked life.

I heard this account from Mr. Rochester on an evening which we spent together in conversation. After I had gone up to my room for the night, I turned to thinking of my master's treatment of me. For some weeks his attitude toward me had been less changeable than at first. I never seemed in his way any longer. He did not act with chilling coldness toward me. When he met me unexpectedly, the meeting seemed welcome. He always had a word and sometimes a smile for me. When called by invitation to his presence, I was honored by a warm reception that made me feel I really possessed the power to please him. I felt at times as if he were my relation, rather than my master. Though he was commanding still, I did not mind that. I saw it was his way. So happy, so pleased did I become with this new interest added to life that I ceased to feel lonely. My life seemed richer. My bodily health improved. I gathered flesh and strength.

And was Mr. Rochester now ugly in my eyes? No,

his face was the object I liked best to see. His presence in a room was more cheering than the brightest fire. Yet I had not forgotten his faults. Indeed I could not, for they were not hidden from me. But I believed that he was naturally a better man who had been spoiled by some cruel misfortune.

All this I had thought as I busied myself in my room, preparing to go to bed. I now extinguished my candle and lay down, but I could not sleep.

"Will Mr. Rochester soon leave Thornfield again?" I asked myself. "Mrs. Fairfax said he seldom stayed here longer than a fortnight at a time, and he has now been with us eight weeks. If he does go, the change will be sad. Suppose he should be absent during the spring, summer, and autumn. How joyless sunshine and fine days will seem!"

I hardly know whether I slept or not after this. At any rate, I started wide awake on hearing a peculiar and mournful murmur, which sounded just above me. I wished I had kept my candle burning. The night was drearily dark. I rose and sat up in bed, listening. The sound was hushed.

I tried again to sleep, but my heart beat anxiously. The clock, far down in the hall, struck two. Just then it seemed my door was touched, as if fingers had swept the panels in groping a way along the dark corridor outside. I said, "Who is there?" Nothing answered. I was chilled with fear.

All at once I remembered that it might be Pilot. When the kitchen door chanced to be left open, he frequently found his way up to the threshold of Mr. Rochester's room. I had seen him lying there myself, in the mornings. The idea calmed me somewhat. I lay down. Silence quiets the nerves, and as an unbroken hush now reigned again through the whole house, I began to feel the return of slumber. But it was not fated that I should sleep that night. Hardly had I begun to doze when I was scared wide awake by a spine-chilling happening.

This was a devilish laugh—soft and deep. The head of my bed was near the door, and I thought at first this laughing ghost stood at my bedside. But I rose, looked around, and could see nothing. As I still gazed, the unnatural sound was repeated. I decided that it came from outside the door. My first impulse was to rise and fasten the bolt. My next act was again to cry out, "Who is there?"

Something gurgled and moaned. Before long, steps retreated up the corridor towards the third story staircase. I heard a door open and close, and all was still.

"Was that Grace Poole? And is she possessed with a devil?" thought I. It was impossible now to remain longer by myself. I must go to Mrs. Fairfax. I threw on my frock and shawl. I drew the bolt and opened the door with a trembling hand. There was a candle burning just outside, left on the matting in the gallery. I was surprised at this, but still more was I amazed to find the air quite dim, as if filled with smoke. While looking to the right hand and left, to find from where these blue clouds came, I became further aware of a strong smell of something burning.

Something creaked. It was an open door, and that door was Mr. Rochester's. The smoke rushed in a cloud from there. I thought no more of Mrs. Fairfax. I thought no more of Grace Poole or the laugh. In an instant I was inside the room. Tongues of flame darted round the bed. The curtains were on fire. In the midst of blaze and smoke Mr. Rochester lay stretched motionless in deep sleep.

"Wake! Wake!" I cried. I shook him, but he only murmured and turned. The smoke had overcome him. Not a moment could be lost. The very sheets were kindling. I rushed to his basin and pitcher. Fortunately one was wide and the other deep, and both were filled with water. I caught them up and drenched the bed and its occupant. Then I flew back to my own room, brought my own water jug, soaked the bed again, and succeeded in extinguishing the flames which were devouring it.

The hiss of the quenched fire, the breakage of a pitcher which I had flung from my hand when I had emptied it, and, above all, the splash of the shower bath I had given him roused Mr. Rochester at last. Though it was now dark, I knew he was awake because I heard him thundering forth exclamations at finding himself lying in a pool of water.

"Is there a flood?" he cried.

"No sir," I answered, "but there has been a fire. Do get up. You are quenched now. I will fetch you a candle." I started toward the door.

"In the name of all the devils, is that Jane Eyre?" he demanded. "What have you done with me, witch? Who is in the room besides you? Have you plotted to drown me?"

"I will fetch you a candle, sir, but please get up. Somebody has plotted something. You cannot find out too soon who and what it is."

"There—I am up now, but don't fetch a candle yet. Wait two minutes till I get into some dry garments, if there are any dry ones—yes, here is my dressing gown. Now, come here."

I brought the candle which still remained in the corridor. He took it from my hand, held it up, and examined the bed, all blackened and scorched, the sheets drenched, the carpet swimming in water.

"What is it? And who did it?" he asked.

I briefly related to him what had happened. I told him about the strange laugh I had heard in the corridor, the steps going up to the third story, the smoke and smell of fire which had led me to his room. I told him in what state I had found matters there, and how I had drenched him with all the water I could lay hands on.

He listened very gravely. His face, as I went on, expressed worry more than surprise. He did not immediately speak when I had concluded.

"Shall I call Mrs. Fairfax?" I asked.

"Mrs. Fairfax? No. What the deuce would you call her for? What can she do? Let her sleep."

"Then I will fetch Leah, and wake John and his wife."

"Not at all. Just be still. You have a shawl on? If you are not warm enough, you may take my cloak. Wrap it about you, and sit down in the armchair. There—I will put it on. Now place your feet on the stool, to keep them out of the wet. I am going to leave you a few minutes. I shall take the candle. Remain where you are till I return. Be as still as a mouse. I must pay a visit to the third story. Don't move or call anyone."

He went. I watched the light of his candle moving away. He passed up the corridor very softly and opened the staircase door with as little noise as possible. He shut it after him, and the last ray vanished. I was left in total darkness. I listened for some noise, but heard nothing. A very long time passed. I grew weary. It was cold, in spite of the cloak. I did not see the use of staying, as I was not to wake the house. I was on the point of risking Mr. Rochester's displeasure by disobeying his orders, when the light once more gleamed dimly on the corridor wall, and I heard his bare feet tread the matting. "I hope it is he," thought I, "and not something worse."

He reentered, pale and very gloomy. "I have found it all out," said he, setting his candle down on the washstand. "It is as I thought."

"How, sir?"

He made no reply, but stood with his arms folded, looking on the ground. At the end of a few minutes he inquired in rather a peculiar tone, "I forget whether you said you saw anything when you opened your door."

"No, sir, only the candlestick on the ground."

"But you heard an odd laugh? Have you heard that laugh before or something like it?"

"Yes, sir. There is a woman who sews here, called Grace Poole—she laughs in that way. She is a strange person."

"Just so. Grace Poole—you have guessed it. She is, as you say, strange. Well, I shall think about it. Meantime I am glad that you are the only person, besides myself, who knows about tonight's happening. You are no talking fool. Say nothing about it. I will account for this state of affairs. Now return to your own room. I shall do very well on the sofa in the library for the rest of the night. It is near four. In two hours the servants will be up."

"Good night then, sir," said I, departing.

He seemed surprised, and I was puzzled, as he had just told me to go.

"What!" he exclaimed. "Are you quitting me already, and in that way?"

"You said I might go, sir."

"But not without taking leave, not without a word or two of good will. Why, you have saved my life! Snatched me from a horrible and torturing death! And you walk past me as if we were strangers! At least shake hands."

He held out his hand. I gave him mine. He took it first in one, then in both his own.

"You have saved my life. I have a pleasure in owing you so immense a debt. I cannot say more. I should hate to owe such a debt to anyone else, but with you it is different. I feel no burden in a debt to you, Jane."

He paused and gazed at me. Words trembled on his lips, but his voice was checked.

"Good night again, sir. There is no debt or burden that you owe me for what I have done."

"I knew," he continued, "you would do me good in some way, at some time. My dear rescuer, good night!"

Strange energy was in his voice; strange fire in his look.

"I am glad I happened to be awake," I said, and then I was going.

"What! You *will* go?"

"I am cold, sir."

"Cold? Yes, and standing in a pool! Go then, Jane. Go!" But he still held my hand, and I could not free it. I thought of a way to persuade him.

"I think I hear Mrs. Fairfax move, sir," said I.

"Well, leave me." He relaxed his fingers, and I was gone.

I regained my bed, but never thought of sleep. Till morning dawned I was tossed on a sea where billows of trouble rolled under waves of joy.

7

I both wished and feared to see Mr. Rochester on the day which followed this sleepless night. I wanted to hear his voice again, yet feared to meet his eyes. During the early part of the morning I constantly expected his coming. He was not often in the habit of entering the schoolroom, but he did step in for a few minutes sometimes, and I had the impression that he was sure to visit it that day.

But morning passed just as usual. Nothing happened to interrupt the quiet course of Adele's studies. Only, soon after breakfast I heard some bustle in the neighborhood of Mr. Rochester's room. I could make out Mrs. Fairfax's voice, and Leah's and the cook's—that is, John's wife—and even John's own gruff tones. There were exclamations of "What a mercy master was not burnt in his bed!" "It is always dangerous to keep a candle lit at night." "How lucky that he had presence of mind to think of the waterjug!" "I wonder he waked nobody!" "It is to be hoped he will not take cold with sleeping on the library sofa."

Afterward there followed a sound of scrubbing and setting things in order. When I passed the room in going downstairs to dinner, I saw through the open door that all was again in proper condition except the bed, which was stripped of its hangings. Leah stood up in the window seat, rubbing the panes of glass which had been dimmed with smoke. I was about to speak to her, for I wished to know what account had been given of the affair. But on coming in, I saw a second person in the chamber—a woman sitting on a chair by the bedside, and sewing rings to new curtains. That woman was none other than Grace Poole.

There she sat, looking as usual in her brown woolen gown, her check apron, and cap. She was intent on her work, in which her whole thoughts seemed absorbed. On her hard forehead and in her ordinary features was nothing of the paleness or desperation one would have expected to see marking the face of a woman who had attempted murder. I was amazed. She looked up while I still gazed at her. Nothing betrayed any feeling of guilt on her part. She said, "Good morning, miss," in her usual manner. Taking up another ring and more tape, she went on with her sewing.

"I will put her to some test," thought I.

"Good morning, Grace," I said. "Has anything happened here? I thought I heard the servants all talking together a while ago."

"It's only that the master was reading in his bed last night. He fell asleep with his candle lit, and the curtains got on fire. Fortunately, he awoke before the bedclothes or the woodwork caught, and managed to quench the flame with the water in the pitcher."

"A strange affair!" I said, in a low voice. "Did Mr. Rochester wake nobody? Did no one hear him move?"

She again raised her eyes to me, and this time there was something suspicious in their expression. She seemed to examine me cautiously. Then she answered, "The servants sleep so far off, miss, they would not be likely to hear. Mrs. Fairfax's room and yours are the nearest to master's, but Mrs. Fairfax said she heard nothing. When people get elderly, they often sleep heavy." She paused and then added, "But you are young, miss, and I should say a light sleeper. Perhaps you may have heard a noise?"

"I did," said I, dropping my voice so that Leah, who was still polishing the panes, could not hear me. "At first I thought it was Pilot. But Pilot cannot laugh, and I am certain I heard a laugh, and a strange one."

She took a new needleful of thread, waxed it carefully, threaded her needle with a steady hand, and then observed, with perfect calmness, "It is hardly likely master would laugh, miss, when he was in such danger. You must have been dreaming."

"I was not dreaming," I said with some anger, for her bold coolness provoked me.

"Have you told master that you heard a laugh?" she inquired.

"I have not had the opportunity of speaking to him this morning."

"You did not think of opening your door and looking out into the corridor?" she further asked.

She appeared to be cross-examining me, attempting to draw from me information unawares. The idea struck me that if she discovered I knew or suspected her guilt, she would be playing some of her wicked pranks on me. I thought it advisable to be on my guard.

"On the contrary," said I, "I locked my door."

"Then you are not in the habit of locking your door every night before you get into bed?"

"Fiend!" I thought, "She wants to know my habits, that she may lay her plans accordingly!" However, anger got the better of my caution. I replied sharply, "Till now I have often omitted to lock the door. I did not think it necessary. I was not aware any danger or annoyance was to be dreaded at Thornfield Hall, but in the future I shall take good care to lock my door before I lie down."

"It will be wise to do so," was her answer. "This neighborhood is as quiet as any I know, and I never heard of the Hall being broken into by robbers, though there are hundreds of pounds' worth of silver plate in the plate-closet, as is well known. And you see, for such a large house there are very few servants because master has never lived here much. But I always think it best to be on the safe side. A door is soon fastened, and it is as well to have a lock between one and any mischief that may be about."

I still stood absolutely dumbfounded at her miraculous calmness and self-possession when the cook entered.

"Mrs. Poole," said she, addressing Grace, "the servants' dinner will soon be ready. Will you come down?"

"No, just put my pint of beer and bit of pudding on a tray, and I'll carry it upstairs."

"You'll have some meat?"

"Just a morsel, and a taste of cheese. That's all."

"And the pudding?"

"Never mind it at present. I shall be coming down before teatime. I'll make it myself."

The cook then turned to me, saying that Mrs. Fairfax was waiting for me; so I departed.

I hardly heard Mrs. Fairfax's account of the fire during dinner, so much was I occupied in puzzling my brains over the mystery of Grace Poole. Still more I wondered about the problem of her position at Thornfield. Why had she not been handed over to the police that morning, or at the very least dismissed from her master's service? He had almost as much as declared last night that she was the criminal. What mysterious cause held him from accusing her? Why had he bound me to secrecy? It was strange. A bold and haughty gentleman seemed somehow in the power of one of the lowest of his employees. He was so much in her power that even when she lifted her hand against his life, he dared not openly charge her with the attempt, much less punish her for it.

I was now in the schoolroom. Adele was drawing. I bent over her and directed her pencil. She looked up with a sort of start.

"What is the matter, mademoiselle?" said she. "Your hands are shaking!"

"I am hot, Adele."

She went on sketching. I went on thinking. "Evening approaches," said I to myself as I looked toward the window. "I have never heard Mr. Rochester's voice or footstep in the house today, but surely I shall see him before tonight is over. I am impatient to talk to him."

When dark actually fell and when Adele left me to go and play in the nursery with Sophie, I listened for the bell to ring below. I listened for Leah coming up with a message. I fancied sometimes I heard Mr. Rochester's own step, and I turned to the door, expecting it to open and admit him. The door remained shut. Only darkness came in through the window. Still, it was not late. He often sent for me at seven or eight o'clock, and it was still only six. Surely I should not be disappointed tonight when I had so many things to say to him! I wanted again to introduce the subject of Grace Poole and to hear what he would answer. I wanted to ask him plainly if he really believed it was she who had made last night's murderous attempt. If that was so, I wanted to inquire why he kept her crime a secret.

A step creaked on the stairs at last. Leah made her appearance, but it was only to say that tea was ready in Mrs. Fairfax's room. There I went, glad at least to go downstairs, for I thought that brought me nearer to Mr. Rochester's presence.

"You must want your tea," said the good lady as I joined her. "You ate so little at dinner. I am afraid you are not well today. You look flushed and feverish."

"Oh, I'm quite well! I never felt better."

"Then you must prove it by showing a good appetite. Will you fill the teapot while I finish my knitting?" Having completed her task, she rose to draw the curtain.

"It is fair tonight," said she as she looked through the panes. "On the whole, Mr. Rochester has had a favorable day for his journey."

"Journey! Has Mr. Rochester gone anywhere? I did not know he was out."

"Oh, he set off the moment he had breakfasted! He has gone to the Leas, Mr. Eshton's place, which is ten miles on the other side of Millcote. I believe there is quite a party assembled there, including Lord Ingram, Sir George Lynn, Colonel Dent, and others."

"Do you expect him back tonight?"

"No—nor tomorrow either. I should think he is very likely to stay a week or more. When these fine, fashionable people get together, they are so surrounded by elegance and gaiety and so well provided with all that can please and entertain, they are in no hurry to separate. Gentlemen, especially, are often in request on such occasions, and Mr. Rochester is so talented and lively that I believe he is a general favorite. The ladies are very fond of him, though you would not think his appearance likely to recommend him in their eyes. But I suppose his talents and abilities—and perhaps also his wealth and good blood—make up for any little fault of looks."

"Are there any ladies at the Leas?"

JANE EYRE / 55

"There are Mrs. Eshton and her three daughters—very elegant young ladies indeed. There are also Blanche and Mary Ingram, who are very beautiful women. I saw Blanche six or seven years ago when she was a girl of eighteen. She came here to a Christmas ball and party Mr. Rochester gave. You should have seen the dining room that day. How richly it was decorated! How brilliantly lit up! I should think there were fifty ladies and gentlemen present—all from the best families. Miss Ingram was considered the belle of the evening."

"Did you see her, Mrs. Fairfax? What was she like?"

"Yes, I saw her. The dining room doors were thrown open, and as it was Christmas time, the servants were allowed to assemble in the hall to hear some of the ladies play and sing. Mr. Rochester asked me to come in, and I sat down in a quiet corner and watched them. I never saw a more splendid scene. The ladies were magnificently dressed. Most of them—at least most of the younger ones—looked handsome, but Miss Ingram was certainly the queen."

"And what was she like?" I asked.

"She was tall and carried herself proudly, with her head held high and posture erect. She had a fair and clear complexion, noble features, and eyes rather like Mr. Rochester's, large and black and as brilliant as jewels. Then, too, she had such a fine head of hair, black and so becomingly arranged. She was dressed in pure white. A yellow scarf was passed over her shoulders, hanging in long fringed ends below her knees. She wore a flower in her hair, and it contrasted well with her dark curls."

"She was greatly admired of course, wasn't she?"

"Yes, indeed, and not only for her beauty. She was

one of the ladies who sang. A gentleman accompanied her on the piano. She and Mr. Rochester sang a duet."

"Mr. Rochester? I did not know he could sing."

"Oh! He has a fine bass voice, and an excellent taste for music."

"And Miss Ingram? What sort of voice had she?" I inquired.

"It was very rich and powerful. She sang delightfully, and it was a treat to listen to her. Afterwards she played the piano. I am no judge of music, but Mr. Rochester is, and I heard him say her performance was remarkably good."

"Is this beautiful and talented lady not yet married?"

"It appears not. I fancy neither she nor her sister have very large fortunes. Old Lord Ingram's estates were left almost entirely to the eldest son."

"But I am surprised," said I, "that no wealthy nobleman or gentleman has taken a fancy to her—Mr. Rochester, for instance. He is rich, is he not?"

"True! Yet I should scarcely fancy Mr. Rochester has any idea of that sort. But you are eating nothing. You have scarcely tasted anything since you began tea."

When I was once more alone, I went over the information I had gotten. I looked into my heart and examined its thoughts and feelings.

"Are *you*," I said to myself, "a favorite with Mr. Rochester? Are you gifted with the power of pleasing him? Are you of importance to him in any way? Go! Your foolishness sickens me. How dared you think so? Poor stupid fool! Listen, then, Jane Eyre, to your sentence. Tomorrow place the mirror before you, and carefully draw your own picture in chalk without softening one defect. Don't omit a single unpleasing line or fault! Write under it, *'Portrait of a governess, poor, plain, and alone in the world.'*

"Afterwards take a piece of smooth ivory, which you have ready in your drawing box. Mix your freshest, finest, clearest tints. Choose your most delicate camel-hair brushes. Draw carefully the loveliest face you can imagine. Paint it in your softest shades and sweetest colors according to the description of Blanche Ingram given by Mrs. Fairfax. Call it *'Portrait of Blanche, a talented lady of rank, riches, and beauty.'*

"In the future, whenever you should chance to imagine that Mr. Rochester thinks well of you, take out these two pictures and compare them. Say to yourself that Mr. Rochester might probably win that noble lady's love, if he chose. Is it likely he would waste a serious thought on this poor and insignificant person?

"I'll do it," I decided, and having made up my mind, I grew calm and fell asleep.

Mr. Rochester had been away for over two weeks when the post office delivered a letter to Mrs. Fairfax.

"It is from the master," said she. "Now I suppose we shall know whether we are to expect his return or not."

While she broke the seal and read the letter, I went on taking my breakfast coffee. It was hot, and I told myself that was why a deep blush suddenly rose to my face. I did not choose to consider why my hand shook and why I spilled half of the contents of my cup into my saucer.

"Well, I sometimes think we are too quiet, but we run a chance of being busy enough now, for a little while at least," said Mrs. Fairfax, still holding the note before her spectacles.

Before I permitted myself to ask for an explanation, I tied the string of Adele's pinafore, which happened to be loose. Having helped her also to another bun and filled her mug with milk, I said, as if it made absolutely no difference to me, "Mrs. Fairfax, is Mr. Rochester likely to return soon?"

"Indeed he is. In three days, he says. That will be next Thursday. He won't be alone either. I don't know how many of the fine people at the Leas are coming with him. He sends directions for all the best bedrooms to be prepared, and the library and drawing rooms are to be cleaned out. I am to get more kitchen hands from the George Inn at Millcote and from wherever else I can. The ladies will bring their maids and the gentlemen their valets. We shall have a full house of it." Mrs. Fairfax, having said these words, swallowed her breakfast quickly and hurried away to commence operations.

The following three days were busy enough. I had thought all the rooms at Thornfield beautifully clean and well-arranged, but it appears I was mistaken. Three women came in to help. And such scrubbing, such brushing, such washing of paint and beating of carpets, such taking down and putting up of pictures, such polishing of mirrors, such lighting of fires in bedrooms, such airing of sheets and featherbeds, I never beheld before or since.

At last came the day set for the arrival of the party. Shortly after six in the evening the sound of wheels and the clump of horses' hoofs were heard approaching the house. Standing behind a curtain where I could see without being seen, I looked out the window.

Four riders galloped up the drive, and after them came two open carriages. Fluttering veils and waving plumes filled the vehicles. Two of the horsemen were young, dashing-looking gentlemen. The third was Mr. Rochester on his black horse, Mesrour, with Pilot bounding before him. At his side rode a lady, and he and she were the first of the party. Her purple riding habit almost swept the ground. Her veil streamed long on the breeze, and gleaming through it shone her dark ringlets.

"Miss Ingram!" exclaimed Mrs. Fairfax, and away she hurried to her post below.

For a while all was hustle and bustle. Mrs. Fairfax seemed to be in a dozen places at once, settling the guests in their rooms and providing for their comfort. I had nothing to do with this activity, but I managed to catch a number of glimpses of the visitors as they went about the house.

Shortly before dinner Mrs. Fairfax came into my room and sat down to rest for a few minutes. While we were speaking of the various ladies and gentlemen, I remarked on how attentive Mr. Rochester seemed toward Miss Ingram.

"You said it was not likely they should think of being married," said I, "but you see Mr. Rochester evidently prefers her to any of the other ladies."

"Yes, I suppose he does admire her."

"And she admires him," I added. "I wish I could see her close at hand. I have not yet had the opportunity."

"You will see her this evening," answered Mrs. Fairfax. "I happened to remark to Mr. Rochester how much Adele wished to be introduced to the ladies. In reply he said, 'Oh, let her come into the drawing room after dinner. Request Miss Eyre to come with her.'"

"Yes, he must have said that from mere politeness. I am sure that I need not go," I remarked.

"Well," answered Mrs. Fairfax, "I told him that you were not used to company, and that I did not think you would like appearing before such a gay party—and all of them strangers to you. But he replied in his quick way, 'Nonsense! If she objects, tell her it is my particular wish. If she refuses, say I shall come and fetch her.'"

"I will not give him that trouble," I answered. "I will go, but I don't like it. Shall you be there, Mrs. Fairfax?"

"No. I begged off, and he accepted my plea. I'll tell you how to manage so as to avoid the embarrassment of coming into the midst of the guests and having to be introduced, which is the most disagreeable part of the whole business. You must go into the drawing room while it is empty, before the ladies leave the dinner table. Choose your seat in any quiet nook you like. You need not stay long after the gentlemen come in, unless you wish to do so. Just let Mr. Rochester see you are there and then slip away. Nobody will notice you."

Following Mrs. Fairfax's advice, I went early to the drawing room, taking Adele with me. We had just seated ourselves when the ladies of the party entered, having left the gentlemen to their after-dinner smoke.

There were only eight; yet somehow as they came in, they gave the impression of a much larger number. Some of them were very tall, many were dressed in white, and all looked like such great ladies in their rich clothing that I felt very small and plain indeed. I rose and curtseyed to them. One or two bent their heads in return. The others only stared at me. Wishing to observe these ladies without attracting too much atten-

tion to myself, I sat down in a seat where I was out of
the way.

First, there was Mrs. Eshton with two of her daughters. She had evidently been a handsome woman and
was good-looking still. Her daughters, Amy and Louise,
were fair as lilies.

Lady Lynn was a large and stout person of about
forty. Very stiff and very haughty-looking, she was richly
dressed in a satin robe. Her dark hair shone glossily
under a band of gems.

Mrs. Dent was less showy, but more ladylike. Her
black satin dress, her scarf of rich foreign lace, and her
pearl ornaments pleased me better than the fancy appearance of Lady Lynn.

But the three most distinguished were the Lady Ingram and her daughters, Blanche and Mary. I looked at

Blanche, of course, with special interest. First, I wished to see whether her appearance agreed with Mrs. Fairfax's description; secondly, whether she at all resembled the picture I had painted of her from imagination; and thirdly, whether she were likely to suit Mr. Rochester's tastes.

In many ways she resembled both my picture and Mrs. Fairfax's description. The noble posture, the fair complexion, and the black hair were all there—but her face? Her face was proud and haughty in expression. She laughed continually. Yet her laugh was full of scorn and sarcasm, as if she were constantly amused by the mistakes and faults of others.

She began discussing botany with the gentle Mrs. Dent. It seemed that Mrs. Dent had not studied that science although, as she said, she liked flowers. Miss Ingram knew a great deal about the subject and delighted in making a show of Mrs. Dent's ignorance and her own cleverness. Then she played the piano; her touch was brilliant. She sang; her voice was fine. She spoke French to her mother; and she spoke it well, with smoothness and a good accent.

And did I now think Miss Ingram such a choice as Mr. Rochester would be likely to make? I could not tell —I did not know his taste in female beauty. If he liked the queenly, she was the very type of queenliness. Besides, she was lively and talented. I thought that most gentlemen would admire her. I already suspected that he *did* admire her. It remained only to see them together for me to be sure what Mr. Rochester thought of her.

I had not long to wait. At last coffee was brought in, and the gentlemen were called. As they entered, I could not help but compare my master with his guests. No doubt most people would have called the other gentlemen attractive, handsome, and imposing, while they would have said that Mr. Rochester's features looked stern and harsh. As for me, when I saw the others smile and laugh, it was nothing. The light of the candles had as much importance as their laugh. When I saw Mr. Rochester smile, his stern features softened and his eyes grew both brilliant and gentle. He was talking at the moment to Louisa and Amy Eshton. I wondered to see them receive his look so calmly. I expected their eyes to fall, their cheeks to blush. Yet I was glad when I found they did not.

"He is not to them what he is to me," I thought. "He is not of their kind. I believe he is of mine. I am sure he is. I understand the language of his expression and movements. Though rank and wealth separate us, I have something in my brain and heart that binds me mentally to him."

Coffee was served. The ladies, after the gentlemen entered, became lively as larks. Conversation grew brisk and merry. Colonel Dent and Mr. Eshton argued on politics while their wives listened. Lady Lynn and Lady Ingram chatted together. Sir George Lynn stood before their sofa with a coffee cup in his hand, and occasionally put in a word. Mr. Frederick Lynn had taken a seat beside Mary Ingram, and was showing her pictures in a book. The tall Lord Ingram leaned with folded arms over the chair of the lively Amy Eshton. Henry Lynn had taken possession of a footstool at the feet of Louisa. Adele was sharing it with him. He was trying to talk in French with the child while Louisa laughed at his blunders. With whom would Blanche Ingram pair? She was standing alone at the table, bending gracefully over an album. She seemed waiting to be approached, but she did not wait too long.

Mr. Rochester was standing near the piano. She walked toward him and sat down on the piano bench. After calling Adele to her side, she said, "Mr. Rochester, I thought you were not fond of children."

"I am not."

"Then what led you to take charge of such a little doll as this?" She pointed to Adele. "Where did you pick her up?"

"I did not pick her up. She was left on my hands."

"You should have sent her to school."

"I could not afford it. Schools are so dear."

"Why, I suppose you have a governess for her. I saw a person with her just now. Has she gone? Oh, no! There she is. You pay her, of course. I should think it quite as expensive—or even more so."

"I have not considered the subject," said he.

"No, you men never do consider economy or common sense. You should hear Mama on the subject of governesses. Mary and I have had a dozen at least in our day. Half of them were hateful and the rest were ridiculous, and *all* of them were horrors—were they not, Mama?"

"My dearest, don't mention governesses. The word makes me nervous. How I have suffered from the worthless creatures! I thank Heaven I have now done with them!"

At this Mrs. Dent bent over to the lady and whispered something in her ear. I suppose it was a reminder that one of those "worthless creatures" was present.

"What of it!" said her ladyship. "I hope it may do her good!" Then she remarked in a lower tone, but still loud enough for me to hear, "I noticed her. I am a judge of faces, and in hers I see all the faults of her class."

"What are they, madam?" inquired Mr. Rochester.

"I will tell you privately," replied she, nodding her head three times to emphasize the importance of this precious information.

"But my curiosity has raised an appetite," insisted my master. "It craves food now."

"Ask Blanche. She is nearer to you than I."

"Oh, don't tell him to ask me, Mama! I have just one word to say of the whole tribe of governesses. They are a nuisance. Not that I ever suffered much from them. I took care to turn the tables. What tricks Theodore and I used to play on Miss Wilson and Mrs. Gray and Madame Joubert! Mary was always too sleepy to join in with spirit. The best fun was with Madame Joubert. Miss Wilson was a poor sickly thing, not worth our trouble. Mrs. Gray was dull and stupid. Nothing took effect on her. But poor Madame Joubert! I see her yet in her rage when we had driven her to extremes. We spilled our tea, crumbled our bread and butter, tossed our books up to the ceiling, and played a serenade with the ruler and desk and fire irons. Theodore, do you remember those merry days?"

"Yes, to be sure I do," replied Lord Ingram. "The poor old stick used to cry out in her awful English, 'Oh, you villains childs!' And then we scolded her for attempting to teach such clever ones as we were, when she was herself so ignorant."

Amy Eshton joined in with her soft, babyish tone, "Louisa and I used to tease our governess too, but she was such a good creature, she would bear anything. Nothing put her out. She was never cross with us. Was she, Louisa?"

"No, never. We might do what we pleased. We used to go through her desk and her workbox, and turn her belongings inside out. But she was so good-natured, she would give us anything we asked for."

It was not Miss Ingram's habit to let anyone else lead the conversation. "I suppose now," said she, "we shall have to hear the history of all the governesses in existence. In order to avoid that, I make a motion to introduce a new topic. Mr. Rochester, do you second my motion?"

"Madam, I am with you on this point as on every other."

"Then mine is the job of changing the topic," said Blanche. "Prince Edward, are you in good voice tonight?"

"Queen Blanche, if you command it, I will be."

"Then, Prince, I order you to polish up your voice, as it will be wanted on my royal service."

Miss Ingram now seated herself with proud grace at the piano. She began playing beautifully and talking meantime. She appeared to be on her high horse tonight. Both her words and her air seemed intended to excite not only the admiration but the amazement of her listeners. She was evidently bent on striking them as something very daring and dashing indeed.

"Oh, I am sick of the young men of the present day!" exclaimed she, while rattling away at the piano. "Poor things, they are not fit to stir a step outside Papa's courtyard gates, nor even to go so far without Mama's permission! They are *so* careful about their pretty faces and white hands and small feet. As if a man had anything to do with beauty! I admit that an ugly *woman* is a poor thing, but as to the *gentlemen*, let them be eager to possess only strength and courage. Let their motto be:—*Hunt, shoot, and fight; the rest is not worth a button.*

"When I marry," she continued, "I am determined my husband shall not rival me in handsomeness. I will permit no competitor near my throne. I shall demand an undivided worship. His attention shall not be shared between me and the shape he sees in his mirror. Mr. Rochester, now sing, and I will play for you."

"I am ready," was the response.

"Now is my time to slip away," thought I, but the tones that then rang upon the air stopped me. Mrs. Fairfax had said Mr. Rochester possessed a fine voice. It was indeed a mellow, powerful bass, into which he threw all his feeling. His voice found a way through the ear to the heart. I waited till the last deep and full note had finished. I then left my corner and made my exit by the side door, which was fortunately near. From there a narrow passage led into the hall. In crossing it, I noticed my sandal was loose. I stopped to tie it, kneeling down for that purpose on the mat at the foot of the staircase. I heard the dining room door open. A gentleman came out. Rising hastily, I stood face to face with him. It was Mr. Rochester.

"How do you do?" he asked.

"I am very well, sir."

"Why did you not come and speak to me in the room?" he questioned.

I thought I might have asked the same question of him, but I would not take that freedom. I answered, "I did not wish to disturb you, as you seemed occupied, sir."

"What have you been doing during my absence?"

"Nothing particular. Teaching Adele as usual."

"You have been getting a good deal paler than you were," he declared. "I saw that at first sight. What is the matter?"

"Nothing at all, sir."

"Did you take cold that night you half drowned me?" he asked.

"Not the least."

"Return to the drawing room," he ordered. "You are leaving too early."

"I am tired, sir."

He looked at me for a minute. "And you are a little unhappy," he said. "What about? Tell me."

"Nothing—nothing, sir. I am not unhappy."

"But I am sure that you are. A few more words would bring tears to your eyes. Indeed, they are there now, shining and swimming. If I had time, I would like to find out what all this means. Well, tonight I excuse you, but understand that so long as my visitors stay, I expect you to appear in the drawing room every evening. It is my wish. Don't neglect it. Now go, and send Sophie for Adele. Good night, my—" He stopped, bit his lip, and abruptly left me.

9

For days Thornfield Hall was the scene of gay activity. Mr. Rochester spent every moment in the entertainment of his guests until one morning he was called to Millcote on business. Then, since he and Miss Ingram had been the life and soul of the party, a noticeable dullness seemed to steal over the spirits of his guests.

That afternoon was wet. It was therefore necessary to postpone a walk the party had proposed to take to see a Gypsy camp nearby. Some of the gentlemen went to the stables. The younger ones, together with the younger ladies, played billiards in the game room. Lady Ingram and Lady Lynn amused themselves with a quiet game of cards. Blanche Ingram threw herself on a sofa and prepared to read during the tiresome hours of Mr. Rochester's absence. The house was silent except for the merriment of the billiard players.

It was approaching evening, and the clock had already given warning of the dinner hour, when little Adele exclaimed, "Oh, there is Monsieur Rochester coming back!" She looked out the drawing-room window.

I turned, and Miss Ingram darted forward from the sofa. The others, too, looked up, for at the same time a crunching of wheels and a splashing tramp of horses' hoofs on the wet gravel could be heard. A closed carriage was approaching.

"Why on earth is he coming home like that?" said Miss Ingram. "He rode Mesrour when he went out, and

70

Pilot was with him. What has he done with the animals?"

As she said this, she approached so near the window that I was obliged to bend back almost to the breaking of my spine. In her eagerness she did not notice me at first, but when she did, she curled her lip and moved away. The carriage stopped before the door. The driver rang the bell, while a gentleman got out. It was not Mr. Rochester, but a tall, fashionable-looking man who was a stranger to me.

"You tiresome monkey!" cried Miss Ingram to Adele. "Who perched you up in the window to give false alarms?" She cast an angry glance at me as if I were at fault.

Soon the newcomer entered. He bowed to Lady Ingram, as the eldest lady present.

"It appears, madam," said he, "that I come at a time when my friend, Mr. Rochester, is away from home. But I arrive from a very long journey, and I think that as an old friend of his I may take the liberty of making myself at home here till he returns."

His manner was polite. When he spoke, his accent struck me as not exactly foreign, but still not altogether English. His age might have been about Mr. Rochester's —between thirty and forty.

It was not till after dinner that I saw him again. He then seemed quite at his ease. Two or three of the gentlemen sat near him, and I caught scraps of their conversation across the room. I presently gathered that the newcomer was called Mr. Mason. Then I learned that he had just arrived in England, and that he came from some hot country. Doubtless, this was the reason that he sat so near the fire and wore a heavy coat in the house. Next he mentioned that his home was in the

West Indies, and I was surprised to hear him tell that it was there he first met Mr. Rochester. He spoke of his friend's dislike of the burning heats, the hurricanes, and rainy seasons of that region. I knew Mr. Rochester had been a traveler, but I thought he had only been on the continent of Europe. Till now I had never heard a hint of visits to more distant shores.

I was considering these things when something broke the thread of my thoughts. Mr. Mason, shivering as someone chanced to open the door, asked for more coal to be put on the fire. The footman who brought the coal stopped near Mr. Eshton's chair and said something to him in a low voice. I heard only the words "old woman" and "quite troublesome."

"Tell her she shall be put in jail if she does not go away," replied Mr. Eshton, who was a county judge.

"No—stop!" interrupted Colonel Dent. "Don't send her away, Eshton. We might have some fun. Better consult the ladies." And speaking out loudly, he continued, "Ladies, you talked of going to visit the Gypsy camp. Sam, here, says that one of the old witches is in the servants' hall at this moment, and insists upon being brought in before us to tell our fortunes. Would you like to see her?"

"Surely, colonel," cried Lady Ingram, "you would not encourage such a low cheat? Dismiss her, by all means, at once!"

"But I cannot persuade her to go away, my lady," said the footman, "nor can any of the servants. Mrs. Fairfax is with her now, begging her to be gone, but she has taken a chair in the chimney corner and says she will not stir from it until she gets leave to come in here."

"What does she want?" asked Mrs. Eshton.

" 'To tell the gentry their fortunes,' she says, ma'am. She swears she must and will do it."

"What is she like?" inquired Amy Eshton.

"A shockingly ugly old creature, miss," declared the footman.

"Why, she's a real witch!" cried Frederick Lynn. "Let us have her in, of course."

"To be sure," agreed his brother. "It would be a thousand pities to throw away such a chance of fun."

"My dear boys, what are you thinking about?" exclaimed Mrs. Lynn.

"I cannot possibly allow any such proceedings," insisted Lady Ingram.

"Indeed, Mama, but you can—and will," pronounced the haughty voice of Blanche Ingram. "I am curious to hear my fortune told. Therefore, Sam, order the old woman in."

"My darling Blanche! Think—" cried her mother.

"I do. I think of everything you can suggest, but I must have my will. Quick, Sam!"

"Yes—yes—yes!" cried all the younger ladies and gentlemen. "Let her come. It will be excellent sport!"

The footman still lingered. "She looks such a rough one," said he.

"Go!" cried Miss Ingram, and the man went.

Excitement instantly seized the party. All the ladies and gentlemen were laughing and jesting when Sam returned.

"She won't come now," said he. "She says it's not her intention to appear before a crowd. I must show her into a room by herself, and then those who wish to consult her must go to her one by one."

"You see now, my queenly Blanche," began Lady Ingram, "she is taking advantage of you. Be warned, my angel girl, and—"

"Show her into the library, of course," cut in the "angel girl." Blanche tossed her head haughtily. "It is not my intention to listen to her before a crowd, either. I mean to have her all to myself. Is there a fire in the library?"

"Yes, ma'am, but she looks such a terror—"

"Cease that chatter, blockhead, and do as you're told," she cried.

Again, Sam vanished, and our feeling of mystery, excitement, and expectation rose once more.

"She's ready now," announced the footman as he reappeared. "She wishes to know who will be her first visitor."

"I think I had just better look in upon her before any of the ladies go," said Colonel Dent.

"Tell her, Sam, a gentleman is coming."

Sam went and returned.

"She says, sir, that she'll have no gentlemen. They need not trouble to come near her, nor any ladies either, except the young and single."

"By Jove, she has taste!" exclaimed Henry Lynn.

Miss Ingram rose seriously. "I go first," she said in a tone as if she were leading a charge in battle.

"Oh, my best! Oh, my dearest! Stop—think!" was her mother's cry. But she swept past in stately silence, passed through the door which Colonel Dent held open, and entered the library.

The minutes passed very slowly. Fifteen were counted before the library door again opened. Miss Ingram returned to us through the arch.

Would she laugh? Would she take it as a joke? All eyes met her with a glance of eager curiosity. She looked neither disturbed nor merry. She walked stiffly to her seat and took it in silence.

"Well, Blanche?" said Lord Ingram.

"What did she say, sister?" asked Mary.

"What do you think? How do you feel? Is she a real fortune teller?" demanded Louisa Eshton.

"Now, now, good people," returned Miss Ingram, "don't press upon me. Really you are easily excited. You seem absolutely to believe we have a genuine witch in the house. I have seen a Gypsy vagabond who has told me what such people usually tell. My curiosity is satisfied, and now I think Mr. Eshton will do well to put the hag in jail tomorrow morning as he threatened."

Miss Ingram took a book, leaned back in her chair, and so refused further conversation. I watched her for nearly half an hour. During all that time she never turned a page, and every moment her face grew darker, more dissatisfied, and more sour with disappointment. She had obviously not heard anything to her advantage.

Meantime, Mary Ingram and Amy and Louisa Eshton declared they dared not go alone, and yet they all wished to go. With great difficulty permission was at last secured from the woman to visit her in a group.

Their call on the Gypsy was not as quiet as Miss Ingram's had been. We heard giggling and little shrieks proceeding from the library. At the end of about twenty minutes they burst the door open and came running across the hall as if they were half scared out of their wits.

"I'm sure she is something not right!" they cried, one and all. "She told us such things! She knows all about us!" They sank breathlessly into the various seats the gentlemen hastened to bring them.

Pressed for further explanation, they declared she had told them of things they had said and done when they were mere children. She had described books and ornaments they had in their rooms at home and keepsakes that different relations had presented to them. They said that she had even read their thoughts and had whispered in the ear of each the name of the person she liked best in the world.

In the midst of the excitement, and while my eyes and ears were fully occupied with the scene before me, I heard a sound at my elbow. I turned and saw Sam.

"If you please, miss, the Gypsy declares that there is another young single lady in the room who has not been to her yet, and she swears she will not go until she has seen all. I thought it must be you. There is no one else. What shall I tell her?"

"Oh, I will go by all means," I answered. I was glad

of the unexpected opportunity to satisfy my excited curiosity. I slipped out of the room, unobserved by any eye, for the company were gathered around the trembling trio just returned.

"If you like, miss," said Sam, "I'll wait in the hall for you. If she frightens you, just call and I'll come in."

"No, Sam, return to the kitchen. I am not in the least afraid." Nor was I, but I was a good deal interested and excited.

The library looked peaceful enough as I entered it, and the woman was seated snugly enough in an easy chair at the chimney corner. She had on a red cloak and a broad-brimmed hat, tied down with a striped handkerchief under the chin. An extinguished candle stood on the table. She was bending over the fire and seemed to be reading in a little black book, like a prayer book, by the light of the blaze. She muttered the words to herself, as many old women do, while she read. She did not cease immediately on my entrance. It appeared that she wished to finish a paragraph.

Finally she shut her book and slowly looked up. The brim of her hat shaded her face; yet I could see as she raised it that it was a strange one. It looked all brown and black. Her hair fell untidily from beneath a white band which passed under her chin and came half over her cheeks.

"Well, and you want your fortune told?" she said in a voice as harsh as her features.

"I don't care about it, Mother. You may please yourself, but I ought to warn you that I have no faith in such foolishness."

"It's impudent of you to say so. But I expected it of you. I heard it in your footstep as you crossed the threshold."

"Did you? You've a quick ear."

"I have; and a quick eye, and a quick brain."

"You need them all in your trade."

"I do, and especially when I have customers like you to deal with. Why don't you tremble?"

"I'm not cold."

"Why don't you turn pale?"

"I'm not sick."

"Why don't you ask to be told your fortune?"

"I'm not silly."

The old woman laughed to herself. She then drew out a short black pipe, and lighting it, began to smoke. Having enjoyed this for a while, she raised her bent body, took the pipe from her lips, and said very slowly, "You are cold, you are sick, and you are silly."

"Prove it," I replied.

"I will, in a few words. You are cold, because you are alone. No one lights the fire that is in you. You are sick, because love, which is the best of feelings, keeps far away from you. You are silly, because you will not try to make love come to you nor will you take one step to meet it where it waits for you."

She again put her short black pipe to her lips and continued her smoking with much energy.

"You might say all that," I replied, "to almost anyone who, you knew, lived as a lonely employee in a great house like this."

"I might say it to almost anyone, but would it be true of almost anyone?"

"In my position?"

"Yes, just so, in *your* position. Find me another one who is in exactly your position."

"It would be easy to find you thousands."

"You could scarcely find me one. If you knew it, you

are very near happiness. Yes, you are within reach of it."

"I don't understand," I said. "I never could guess a riddle in my life."

"If you wish me to speak more plainly, show me your palm."

"And I must cross it with silver, I suppose?" I asked.

"To be sure."

I gave her a shilling. She put it into an old stocking foot which she took out of her pocket. Having tied it round and replaced it, she told me to hold out my hand. I did. She brought her face near to the palm and studied it without touching it.

"It is too fine," said she. "I can make nothing of such a hand as that, almost without lines. Besides, what is in a palm? The future is not written there."

"I believe you," said I.

"No," she continued, "it is in the face. It is on the forehead, about the eyes, in the eyes themselves, in the lines of the mouth. Kneel and lift up your head."

I knelt within half a yard of her. She stirred the fire, so that a ripple of light broke from the disturbed coals. The glare, however, only threw her face into deeper shadow. Mine it lighted up.

"I wonder with what feelings you came to me tonight," she said when she had examined me awhile. "I wonder what thoughts are busy in your heart during all the hours you sit in these rooms with the fine people passing before you."

"I feel tired often, sleepy sometimes, but seldom sad."

"Are you then secretly hoping for something or expecting something pleasing to happen in the future?" the woman asked.

"Not I. The most I hope for is to save enough money out of my earnings to set up a school some day in a little house rented by myself."

"Bah! That is a poor hope for one to live on. When you sit in that window seat, do you ever—"

"Stop!" I cried. "How do you know my habits? How do you know that I am accustomed to sit in the window seat? Have you learned it from the servants?"

"Ah! You think yourself clever! Well, perhaps I have. To speak the truth, I have an acquaintance with one of them—Mrs. Poole—"

I started to my feet when I heard the name.

"You have, have you?" I exclaimed. "There is the devil in this business, after all, then!"

"Don't be alarmed," continued this strange being. "She's a safe one, is Mrs. Poole. She's close and quiet. Anyone may put confidence in her. But, as I was saying, when you are sitting in your window seat, do you think of nothing but your future school? Have you no interest in any of the company in this house? Is there not one face you look at especially? Is there not one person whose movements you like to follow with particular attention?"

"I like to look at them all," I said.

"But do you never single out one or two from the rest? Perhaps there are a particular lady and gentleman whom you watch most closely?"

"When the actions or looks of a pair seem to tell me a tale, it amuses me to watch them."

"What sort of tale do you like to hear?" the old Gypsy asked.

"Oh, I have not much choice! They are generally on the same subject—courtship and marriage."

"And do you like that subject?"

"Positively not. I don't care about it. It is nothing to me."

"Nothing to you? When another young lady sits and smiles in the eyes of a gentleman you think well of, it is nothing to you?"

"I don't know the gentlemen here. I have exchanged scarcely a word with them. As to thinking well of them, I consider some respectable and stately and middle-aged, and others young, handsome, and lively. But certainly they are all at liberty to receive whatever smiles they please without its concerning me in the least."

"You don't know the gentlemen here? Will you say that of the master of the house?" the woman asked.

"He is not at home," I said.

"You avoid giving an answer to my question! He went to Millcote this morning and will be back here tonight or tomorrow. Does that put him off the list of your acquaintances?"

"No, but I can scarcely see what Mr. Rochester has to do with the subject you were discussing."

"I was talking of ladies smiling into the eyes of gentlemen," said the strange old woman. "Haven't you noticed any lady smiling at Mr. Rochester?"

"Mr. Rochester has the right to enjoy the company of his guests," I told her. The strange talk, voice, and manner of the Gypsy had by this time made me feel as if I were dreaming. One unexpected sentence came from her lips after another, till I wondered whether she had been looking deeply into my heart and watching its workings.

"Can you tell me," I asked, "whether Mr. Rochester is to be married?"

"Yes—to the beautiful Miss Ingram."

"Shortly?"

"It is more than likely," she replied. "Surely he must love such a handsome, noble, witty, talented lady. And probably she loves him, or at least his purse. I know she is greatly interested in Mr. Rochester's fortune, for she asked me several questions about it. When I told her it was considerably smaller than she thought, the corners of her mouth fell half an inch. Mr. Rochester had better look out. If another comes along with a larger estate, he's dished—"

"But, Mother, I did not come to hear Mr. Rochester's fortune. I came to hear my own, and you have told me nothing about it."

"Your fortune is yet doubtful. Fate has set for you a measure of happiness; that I know. I knew it before I came here this evening. Fate has laid your share carefully on one side for you. It depends on you to stretch out your hand and pick it up. But enough! I have finished. Go, Miss Eyre. Leave me. This play is played out."

Where was I? Did I wake or sleep? Had I been dreaming? Did I dream still? The old woman's voice had changed. It was now as familiar to me as the sound of my own. I got up, but did not go. I looked at her. Then I stirred the fire and looked again. But she drew her bonnet and band closer about her face, and again motioned me to depart. The flame lighted her hand as it was stretched out. Being now on the alert, I at once noticed that hand. It was no more the wrinkled limb of an aged person than my own. A broad ring flashed on the little finger. Stooping forward, I looked at it and saw a gem I had seen a hundred times before. Again I looked at the face, which was no longer turned from me. On the contrary, the bonnet and band were taken off, and now the entire head of this unusual woman appeared.

"Well, Jane, do you know me?" asked a familiar voice.

"Only take off the red cloak, sir, and then—"

"But the string is in a knot. Help me."

"Break it, sir."

"There, then!" And Mr. Rochester stepped out of his disguise.

"Now, sir, what a strange idea!"

"But well carried out, eh? Don't you think so?"

"With the other ladies you must have managed well," I said.

"But not with you?"

"You scarcely acted the part of a Gypsy with me, sir."

"What part did I act? My own?"

"No. I believe that you have been purposely trying to make me tell what is in my mind. It is hardly fair, sir."

"Do you forgive me, Jane?"

"I cannot tell till I have thought it over. If I decide, on thinking it over, that I have not made myself look foolish, I shall try to forgive you. Nevertheless, it was not right."

"Oh! You have said nothing to give yourself away. You have been very careful and very sensible."

I thought to myself that I had been on my guard almost from the beginning. I knew fortune tellers did not talk as this one had. Besides, I had noticed her counterfeit voice and how anxious she was to conceal her features. But my mind had been running to Grace Poole —that living puzzle, that mystery of mysteries, as I considered her. I had never thought of Mr. Rochester as being connected with the Gypsy woman.

"Well," said he, "what are you thinking about? What does that grave smile mean?"

"It means that I am full of wonder, sir. I have your permission to go now, I suppose?"

"No, stay a moment."

"I had better not stay long, sir. It must be near eleven o'clock. Oh! Are you aware, Mr. Rochester, that a stranger has arrived since you left this morning?"

"A stranger! No. Who can it be? I expected no one. Has he gone?"

"No. He said he had known you a long time, and that he would take the liberty of making himself at home here till you returned."

"The devil he did! Did he give his name?"

"His name is Mason, sir. And he comes from the West Indies—from Spanish Town in Jamaica, I think."

Mr. Rochester was standing near me. He had taken my hand as if to lead me to a chair. As I spoke, he gave my wrist a sudden grip. The smile on his lips froze.

"Mason!—the West Indies!" he said. "Mason—the West Indies!" he repeated, and he went over the words three times, growing whiter than ashes. He hardly seemed to know what he was doing.

"Do you feel ill, sir?" I inquired.

"Jane, I've got a blow—I've got a blow, Jane!" He staggered as if he had actually been struck.

"Oh! Lean on me, sir," I cried.

"Jane, you offered me your shoulder once before. Let me have it now."

"Yes, sir, yes; and my arm."

He sat down and made me sit beside him. Holding my hand in both his own, he pressed it. At the same time, he gazed at me with the most troubled look.

"My little friend!" said he. "I wish I were in a quiet island with only you; and with all trouble, danger, and ugly memories removed from me."

"Can I help you, sir? I'd give my life to serve you."

"Jane, if help is wanted, I'll seek it at your hands. I promise you that."

"Thank you, sir. Tell me what to do, I'll try, at least, to do it."

"Fetch me now, Jane, a glass of wine from the dining room. They will be at supper there. Tell me if Mason is with them, and what he is doing."

I went. I found all the party in the dining room at supper, as Mr. Rochester had said. They were not seated at the table. The supper was arranged on the sideboard. Each had taken what he chose and they stood about here and there in groups, their plates and glasses in their hands. Everyone seemed in high glee. Laughter and conversation were going on everywhere. Mr. Mason stood near the fire, talking to Colonel and Mrs. Dent, and appeared as merry as any of them. I filled a wine glass. As I did so, I saw Miss Ingram look at me frowningly. She thought I was taking a liberty, I daresay. When I returned to the library, Mr. Rochester's extreme paleness had disappeared, and he looked once more firm and stern. He took the glass from my hand.

"Here is to your health, my good angel!" he said. He swallowed the contents and returned it to me. "What are they doing, Jane?"

"Laughing and talking, sir."

"They don't look grave and mysterious, as if they had heard something strange?" he asked.

"Not at all. They are full of jests and gaiety."

"And Mason?"

"He was laughing too."

"If all these people came into the room to spit upon me, what would you do, Jane?"

"Turn them out of the room, sir, if I could."

He half smiled. "But what if I were to go to them,

and they only looked at me coldly and whispered scornfully among themselves and then left me one by one? Would you go with them?"

"I rather think not, sir. I should have more pleasure in staying with you."

"To comfort me?"

"Yes, sir, to comfort you as well as I could."

"Go back now into the room," ordered my master. "Step quietly up to Mason, and whisper into his ear that Mr. Rochester has come and wishes to see him. Show him in here and then leave me."

"Yes, sir."

I did his bidding. The company all stared at me as I passed straight among them. I delivered the message to Mr. Mason and led him from the room. I ushered him into the library, and then I went upstairs.

At a late hour, after I had been in bed some time, I heard the visitors go to their rooms. I distinguished Mr. Rochester's voice and heard him say, "This way, Mason. This is your room."

He spoke cheerfully, and his gay tones set my heart at ease. I was soon asleep.

10

I had forgotten to draw my curtain. The result was that when the moon came in her course opposite my window and looked in at me through the uncovered panes, her glorious light awakened me. I half rose and stretched my arm to draw the curtain.

Good heavens! What a cry!

The silence of the night was torn by a savage, sharp, shrill sound that ran from end to end of Thornfield Hall! My pulse stopped. My heart stood still. My outstretched arm was paralyzed. The cry died and was not repeated. Indeed, whoever or whatever uttered that fearful shriek could not soon repeat it. The thing delivering such a yell must rest before it could again make the same effort.

The cry had come out of the third story, for it had seemed overhead. And overhead—yes, in the room just above my ceiling—I now heard a struggle. It seemed to be a deadly one from the noise, and a half-choked voice shouted, "Help! Help! Help!" Then, while the staggering and stamping went on wildly, I heard the words: "Rochester! Rochester! For the love of heaven, come!"

Outside in the corridor a door opened, and someone ran across the floor and up the stairs. Another step stamped on the flooring above and something fell. Then there was silence.

I put on some clothes, though horror shook all my limbs. I hurried from my room. The sleepers were all awakened. Exclamations and terrified murmurs sounded everywhere. Door after door unclosed, and one after another looked out. The corridor filled with the ladies and gentlemen, who had left their beds.

"Oh, what is it?" "Who is hurt?" "What has happened?" "Fetch a light!" "Is it fire?" "Are there robbers?" "Where shall we run?" These cries were raised in confusion on all sides. Except for the moonlight and a few candles, they would have been in complete darkness. They ran to and fro. They crowded together. Some sobbed; some stumbled. The excitement was dreadful.

"Where the devil is Rochester?" cried Colonel Dent. "I cannot find him in his bed."

"Here! Here!" was shouted in return. "Be calm, all of you. I'm coming."

The door at the end of the corridor opened, and Mr. Rochester advanced with a candle. He had just come down from the upper story. One of the ladies ran to him directly and seized his arm. It was Miss Ingram.

"What awful event has taken place?" said she. "Speak! Let us know the worst at once!"

"But don't pull me down or strangle me," he replied, for the two Misses Eshton were hanging upon him now. Also, the two elderly ladies in their night robes and caps were bearing down on him like ships in full sail.

"All's right! All's right!" he cried. "Ladies, keep off, or I shall grow dangerous."

And dangerous he looked. His black eyes darted sparks. Calming himself by an effort, he added, "A servant has had a nightmare. That is all. She's an excitable, nervous person. She imagined her dream to be a ghost or something of that sort, no doubt, and has taken a fit with fright. Now then, I must see you all back into your rooms, for till the house is settled, she cannot be looked after. Gentlemen, have the goodness to set the ladies an example. Miss Ingram, I am sure you will not fail to prove equal to idle terrors. Amy and Louisa, return to your nests like a pair of doves, as you are. Ladies, you will certainly take cold if you stay in this chilly corridor any longer."

Thus, by coaxing and commanding he managed to get them all once more into their rooms. I did not wait to be ordered back to mine, but retreated unnoticed.

I did not return, however, to go to bed. On the contrary, I began to dress myself carefully. The sounds and words after the scream had probably been heard only by me, for they had proceeded from the room above mine. They convinced me that it was not a servant's dream which had thus struck horror through the house, and that the explanation Mr. Rochester had given was merely intended to quiet his guests. I dressed, then, to be ready for emergencies. When dressed, I sat a long time by the window, looking out over the silent grounds and fields, and waiting for I knew not what. It seemed to me that some event must follow the strange cry, struggle, and call.

At last a cautious hand tapped quietly on my door.

"Am I wanted?" I asked.

"Are you up?" said the voice of Mr. Rochester.

"Yes, sir."

"And dressed?"

"Yes."

"Come out, then, quietly."

I obeyed. Mr. Rochester stood in the gallery, holding a light.

"I want you," he said. "Come this way. Take your time, and make no noise."

My slippers were thin. I could walk the matted floor as softly as a cat. He glided up the corridor and up the stairs, stopping in the dark, low hall of the third story. I had followed and stood at his side.

"Have you a sponge in your room?" he asked in a whisper.

"Yes, sir."

"Have you any salts—smelling salts?"

"Yes."

"Go back and fetch both."

I returned, got the sponge from the washstand, the salts from my drawer, and went again to the third floor. Mr. Rochester was still waiting. Approaching one of the small black doors, he put a key in the lock. Then he paused and addressed me again. "You don't turn sick at the sight of blood?"

"I think I shall not, sir. I have never been tested yet." I felt a thrill while I answered him, but no coldness and no faintness.

"Just give me your hand," he said. "It will not do to risk a fainting fit."

I put my fingers into his. "Your hand is warm and steady," was his remark. He turned the key and opened the door.

I saw a room I remembered to have seen the day Mrs. Fairfax showed me the house. The walls were hung with tapestry, which was now pulled back in one section, showing a door which on that first day had been hidden. This door was open, and from the next room I heard a snarling sound, almost like that of an angry dog. Putting down his candle, Mr. Rochester said to me, "Wait a minute." He went into the other room. As he did so, a shout of laughter greeted him. It was loud at first and ended in Grace Poole's own ghostly ha! ha! *She* then was there. He made some sort of arrangement without speaking, though I heard a low voice reply to him. Then he came out and closed the door behind him.

"Come here, Jane!" he called. I walked around to the other side of a large bed, which filled a considerable part of the room. Beside it was an easy chair in which a man sat, completely dressed except for his coat. He was still; his head leaned back; his eyes were closed. Mr. Rochester held the candle over him, and I recognized in his pale and almost lifeless face the stranger, Mason. I saw too that his shirt on one side and on one arm was almost soaked in blood.

"Hold the candle," said Mr. Rochester, and I took it. He fetched a basin of water from the washstand. "Hold that," said he. I obeyed. He took the sponge, dipped it in, and moistened the corpselike face. He asked for my smelling salts and applied them to the man's nostrils. Mr. Mason shortly unclosed his eyes and groaned. Mr. Rochester opened the shirt of the wounded man and

bandaged his arm and shoulder. He sponged away the blood, which kept trickling down fast.

"Is there any immediate danger?" asked Mason.

"Pooh! No—a mere scratch. Don't be so weak, man. Bear up! I'll get a doctor for you now, myself. You'll be able to be removed by morning, I hope. Jane," he continued, turning to me.

"Sir?"

"I shall have to leave you in this room with this gentleman for an hour or two. You will sponge the blood when it returns, as I am doing. If he feels faint, you will put the glass of water on that stand to his lips, and your salts to his nose. You will not speak to him on any account, and, Richard, it will be at the peril of your life if you speak to her. Just open your lips or disturb yourself, and I'll not be responsible for the consequences."

Again the poor man groaned. Fear, either of death or of something else, appeared almost to paralyze him. Mr. Rochester put the bloody sponge into my hand, and I began to use it as he had done. He watched me a second. Then saying, "Remember! No conversation!" he left the room. I experienced a strange feeling as the key turned in the lock, and the sound of his steps passed away.

Here I was on the third floor, locked into one of its mysterious rooms. Night was around me. A pale and bloody sight was under my eyes and hands. A murderous creature was separated from me only by a single door. Yes, the rest I could bear, but the thought of Grace Poole's bursting in upon me made my heart sink.

I must keep my post, however. I must watch this pale face—these blue lips forbidden to open, these eyes now shut, now open, now wandering around the room, now looking at me, and always showing a great horror. I must dip my hand again and again in the basin of blood and water, and wipe away the trickling gore. I must listen for the movements of the wild beast or fiend in the next room. But since Mr. Rochester's visit it seemed to have been quieted. All through this part of the night I heard but three sounds: the creaking of a step, a brief return of the snarling, doglike noise, and a deep human groan.

Then my own thoughts worried me. What mystery was this that broke out, once before in fire and now in blood, at the deadest hours of night? What sort of creature was Grace Poole, who seemed like a devil masked behind a woman's face?

And this man I was caring for—how had he become caught in the web of horror? Why had he been attacked? What had made him come to this part of the house at such an hour when he should have been in bed? I had heard Mr. Rochester lead him to a room on the floor below. What had brought him here? And why, now, did he seem so little angered by what had been done to him? Why did he so quietly agree to hide this deed as Mr. Rochester insisted?

Why *did* Mr. Rochester insist on hiding the deed? His guest had been attacked, and before that his own life had almost been taken. Yet both attempts he kept secret! Furthermore, I saw that Mr. Mason accepted Mr. Rochester's commands without any objection. What then had caused my master's fears when he first heard of Mr. Mason's arrival? Only a few hours ago just the mention of the man's name had fallen on him as a thunderbolt might fall on an oak.

Oh! I could not forget his look and paleness when he whispered, "Jane, I have got a blow—I have got a blow, Jane." I could not forget how the arm which he rested on my shoulder had trembled. It was no light matter which could thus disturb the strong mind of Fairfax Rochester.

"When will he come? When will he come?" I cried to myself as the night went on and on. My bleeding patient was sick and moaning, but neither day nor help arrived. Again and again I held the water to Mason's lips. Again and again I used the smelling salts to keep him from fainting. My efforts seemed useless, for he was fast losing his strength. He moaned so, and looked so weak, wild, and lost, that I feared he was dying. Yet I was not allowed even to speak to him!

At last I saw streaks of gray light at the edges of the window curtains. I knew then that dawn was approaching. Presently I heard Pilot bark far below in the courtyard. In five minutes more the key turning in the lock told me that help had finally come. The time I had waited could not have lasted more than two hours, but many a week has seemed shorter.

Mr. Rochester entered, bringing the doctor. "Now, Carter, be quick about it," he said to the physician. "I give you but half an hour for dressing the wound, fastening the bandages, getting the patient downstairs and all."

"But is he fit to move, sir?"

"No doubt of it. It is nothing serious. He is nervous, and his spirits must be kept up. Come, set to work."

Mr. Rochester drew back the thick curtain and let in all the daylight he could. Then he approached Mason, whom the doctor was already treating.

"Now, my good fellow, how are you?" he asked.

"She's done for me, I fear," was the faint reply.

"Not a whit! Have courage! Two weeks from today

you'll hardly be a pin the worse for it. You've lost a little blood, that's all. Carter, you can tell him there's no danger, can't you?"

"I can do that truthfully," said Dr. Carter, who had now removed the bandages. "Only I wish I could have got here sooner. He would not have bled so much—but how is this? The flesh on the shoulder is torn as well as cut. This wound was not done with a knife. There have been teeth here!"

"She bit me," Mason murmured. "She gashed me like a tigress when Rochester got the knife away from her."

"You should not have yielded. You should have wrestled with her at once," said Mr. Rochester.

"Oh, it was frightful," Mason declared, shuddering. "I did not expect it. She looked so quiet at first."

"I warned you," was his friend's answer. "I said to be on your guard when you go near her. Besides, you might have waited till tomorrow and had me with you. It was foolish to attempt to talk to her tonight, and alone."

"I thought I could have done some good."

"You thought! You thought! Yes, it makes me impatient to hear you. However, you have suffered and are likely to suffer enough for not taking my advice; so I'll say no more. Carter—hurry! hurry! The sun will soon rise, and I must get him away."

"Directly, sir. The shoulder is just bandaged. I must look to this other wound in the arm. She has had her teeth here too, I think."

"She sucked the blood. She said she'd drain my heart," declared Mason.

I saw Mr. Rochester shudder. An expression of disgust, horror, and hatred twisted his face, but he only said, "Come, be silent, Richard, and never mind her nonsense. Don't repeat it."

"I wish I could forget it," was the answer.

"You will when you are out of the country. When you get back to Spanish Town, you may think of her as dead and buried. Or rather, you need not think of her at all."

"It will be impossible to forget this night!" moaned Mason.

"It is not impossible," said Mr. Rochester sternly. "Have some energy, man. You thought you were as dead as a herring two hours ago, and you are all alive and talking now. There! Carter has done with you or nearly so. I'll have you ready to leave in a few moments."

Mr. Rochester glanced at me. "Jane, step out into the hall and listen for anyone moving about the house. Then report to me."

I did as he requested. On returning I announced, "All is very still, sir."

"We shall get away without exciting attention, Dick. It will be better both for your sake and for that of the poor creature in there. Here, Carter, help him on with his coat. Where did you leave your fur cloak, Mason? I know you can't travel a mile without that in this cold climate. Is it in your room? Jane, run down to Mr. Mason's room. It's the one next to mine. Fetch the cloak you will see there."

I ran and returned, carrying an immense overcoat lined and edged with fur.

"Now, I've another errand for you," said my master. "You must go to my room. There you will open the middle drawer of my table and take out a small bottle and a little glass you will find there. Be quick!"

I flew there and back, bringing the required articles.

"That's good!" said Mr. Rochester approvingly. "Now, doctor, I shall take the liberty of giving the patient a dose on my own responsibility. I got this mixture from a fellow who claimed it has magic qualities by means of which a sick man can be made as good as new in a few minutes. I'm sure there is nothing magic or remarkable about it, except that it is very powerful and dangerous, and therefore must be used with great care. It is good on such occasions as this. Jane, a little water."

He held out the tiny glass, and I half filled it from the water bottle on the washstand. He measured twelve drops of a red liquid and presented it to Mason.

"Drink it, Richard. For an hour or so it will give you the heart you lack."

"But will it hurt me?"

"Drink! Drink! Drink it!"

Mr. Mason obeyed because it was evidently useless to refuse. He was now completely dressed to go out. He still looked pale, but he was no longer bloody and stained. Mr. Rochester let him sit for three minutes after he had swallowed the liquid, and then took his arm.

"Now I am sure you can get on your feet," he said. "Try."

The patient rose.

"Carter, take him under the shoulder. Be of good cheer, Richard. Step out! That's it!"

"I do feel better," remarked Mason.

"I am sure you do. Now, Jane, go on before us to the back stairs. Unlock the side door, and tell the driver of the carriage you will see in the yard to be ready. And, Jane, if anyone is about, come to the foot of the stairs and give warning."

I went ahead to do as I had been instructed, and the

gentlemen followed. Mason, supported by Mr. Rochester and the doctor, seemed to walk with reasonable ease. They assisted him into the carriage, and Carter got in beside him.

"Take care of him," said Mr. Rochester to the physician, "and keep him at your house till he is quite well. I shall ride over in a day or two to see how he gets on. Richard, how is it with you?"

"The fresh air revives me, Fairfax."

"Leave the window open on his side, Carter. Good-by, Dick."

"Fairfax!" called the wounded man.

"Well, what is it?" asked Mr. Rochester.

"Let her be taken care of. Let her be treated as tenderly as may be. Let her—" He stopped and burst into tears.

"I am doing my best, and have done it, and will do it," my master answered. He shut the door, and the vehicle drove away.

"How I wish there were an end to all this!" added Mr. Rochester as he closed and barred the heavy yard gates. Having done this, he moved with a slow step towards a door in the wall of the orchard. Since I supposed he had finished with me, I prepared to return to the house. However, I heard him call, "Jane!" He had opened the door and stood by it, waiting for me.

"Come and get some fresh air for a few moments," he said. "That house is a dungeon."

We strolled down a walk which had apple, pear, and cherry trees on one side and a border of all sorts of flowers on the other side. The sun was just beginning to come up in the east and gleamed down upon us.

"Jane, will you have a flower?" He plucked a rose and offered it to me.

"Thank you, sir."

"You have passed a strange night, haven't you, Jane?"

"Yes, sir."

"And it has made you look pale. Were you afraid when I left you alone with Mason?"

"I was afraid that someone would come out of the other room."

"But I had fastened the door, Jane. I had the key in my pocket. I should have been a careless shepherd if I had left my pet lamb unguarded, so near a wolf's den. You were safe."

"Will Grace Poole live here still, sir?"

"Oh, yes! Don't trouble your head about her. Put the thing out of your thoughts."

"Yet it seems to me your life is hardly safe while she stays."

"Never fear. I will take care of myself," he declared calmly.

"When I told you of Mr. Mason's arrival last night, you seemed to fear some danger. Is that peril gone now, sir?"

Mr. Rochester shook his head. "I cannot be sure of that," he said, "till Mason is out of England—and not even then. Jane, I am like a man who has built his house on the edge of a volcano, which may crack and spit fire any day. I cannot be safe from the danger which hangs over me."

"But surely," I cried, "Mr. Mason will never purposely hurt you. He does not seem that sort of man, and you appear to have a strong influence over him."

"You are quite right," Mr. Rochester agreed, "but he might indeed injure me without intending to do so. One careless word from him might deprive me forever of happiness."

"Tell him to be careful, sir," I begged him. "Let him know what you fear, and show him how to avoid the danger."

He laughed bitterly. "If I could do that, silly girl, where would the danger be? I cannot give him orders in this case. There is a shameful thing which I keep locked up in that house. Mason knows what this mystery is, but he does not know that I am keeping it a secret even from my closest friends. Thus at any moment he may make a chance remark that will tell my secret to all my friends and all the world."

"Can you not beg him to say nothing about it, sir?"

"To keep my secret," said Mr. Rochester, "is the one favor which a man like Mason would never do. I must say nothing about it and hope for the best. Being a polite and courteous gentleman, Richard Mason is not likely to go about discussing such an unpleasant subject. Perhaps he will never mention it. But let us talk of other matters." He waved his hand as if to dismiss the topic.

We had come to an arch in the wall, lined with ivy. It contained a wooden seat. Mr. Rochester sat down, leaving room for me beside him. But I still stood before him.

"Sit here," he said. "The bench is long enough for two. You don't hesitate to take a place at my side, do you?"

I answered him by sitting down.

"Now, my little friend," he went on, "I'll put a problem before you. There is a question in my mind which you must help me to answer. Are you willing to listen?"

"Yes, sir, I am always anxious to serve you."

"Well then, Jane, I want you to use your imagination. Suppose that you were no longer a well-brought-up young lady. Suppose that instead you were a wild young

man who had been allowed his own way from childhood on. Imagine yourself in a far-off land. Suppose that
you there make a great mistake, the results of which
cast a dark shadow over your whole life. You are miserable, for hope has left you. You wander here and
there, seeking peace and happiness, but all you find are
a few brief moments of wicked pleasure. Sick at heart,
you come home after years of wandering. You meet a
stranger and find in her those good qualities for which
you had searched many years, and never before had
found. Your friendship with this person is an influence
which makes you wish to get a new start. You feel that
better days, higher wishes, and nobler feelings are returning to you. You desire to live your life in a more
worthy way. *But* there is an obstacle in your path. To
climb over this obstacle, you must do something of
which the world will not approve. In order to take the
first step toward this good life—strangely enough—
you must now for the first time break a law."

"I would never approve of breaking the laws of man
or God," I said. "I cannot believe that good would come
of it."

"But what if the deed would harm no one?" Mr.
Rochester asked.

He waited for an answer. What was I to say? Oh,
for some good spirit to suggest a wise reply! The west
wind whispered in the leaves around me, but its breeze
carried no message. The birds sang in the treetops, but
their song brought me no inspiration.

"How could you be sure that the deed would hurt
nobody?" I asked at last. "Besides, the man who breaks
a law comes closer to evil and so harms himself. Having once broken one law, a man more easily breaks another. From there it is but a step to the condition of the

hardened lawbreaker, who cannot distinguish good from evil or right from wong."

How Mr. Rochester received my words I could not tell. I could read nothing in his face, which remained without expression. His only reply was, "Well, my little friend, we shall see—we shall see." Then his tone changed to a less serious one, and he added, "You have noticed my interest in Miss Ingram. Don't you think, Jane, that if I married her, she would influence me to lead a better life?"

I had no chance to answer this question, for at that moment Mr. Rochester started up, exclaiming, "Bless me! There are Dent and Lynn in the stables! I must speak to them."

As I walked one way, he went in the other direction. I heard him in the yard, saying cheerfully, "Mason got the start of you all this morning. He was gone before sunrise. I rose at four to see him off."

11

After all the visitors left, a quiet time followed in Thornfield Hall. Nothing was said of the master's marriage, and I saw no preparations going on for such an event. Almost every day I asked Mrs. Fairfax if she had yet heard anything decided. Her answer was always "No." She said that once she had actually put the question to Mr. Rochester as to when he was going to bring his bride home, but he had answered her only by a joke and one of his queer looks. She could not tell what to make of him.

One thing especially surprised me, and that was, there were no journeys back and forward, no visits by Mr. Rochester to Ingram Park. To be sure, it was twenty miles off, on the borders of another county. But what was that distance to an eager lover? To so expert a horseman as Mr. Rochester, it would be but a morning's ride. I began to hope that the match had been broken off and that one or both of them had changed their minds. I used to look at my master's face to see if it were sad or angry, but I could not remember the time when it had been so clear of clouds or evil feelings. If, in the moments my pupil and I spent with him, I sank into fits of sadness, he would become gay and would try to cheer me. Never had he called me more often to his presence. Never had he been kinder to me. Alas! Never had I loved him so well.

One summer evening, Adele, who was weary with gathering wild strawberries half the day, went to bed at sunset. I watched her drop asleep, and when I left her, I walked out into the garden.

I strolled awhile alone on the pavement, but the well-known scent of a cigar stole upon me. Although he was nowhere to be seen, I knew that my master was approaching. As I was not anxious to meet Mr. Rochester just now, I moved toward the gate, only to see him entering. I stepped aside, thinking that he would not stay long. If I remained quiet, he would never see me.

But no—the evening was as pleasant to him as to me, and this old garden as attractive. He strolled on. Now he looked at the gooseberry tree branches with their fruit as large as plums. Now he took a ripe cherry from a stem. Now he stooped towards a knot of flowers to smell their fragrance.

"Good! He has his back towards me," thought I, "and he is occupied, too. Perhaps if I walk softly, I can slip away unnoticed."

I walked on the grass so that the crackle of the pebbles might not betray me. He was standing among the flower beds about a yard or two from where I had to pass. "I shall get by very well," I thought.

But as I went by, he said quietly without turning, "Come back, Jane. On so lovely a night it is a shame to sit in the house, and surely no one can wish to go to bed when the sun has barely set."

I was both surprised and embarrassed. Since no excuse came to my mind, I could do nothing but fall in and walk beside him.

"Jane," he began as we slowly walked down in the direction of the great horse-chestnut tree, "Thornfield is a pleasant place in summer, is it not?"

"Yes, sir."

"You have come to like it here, haven't you?"

"I have, indeed."

"And though I can hardly see why, I notice that you have a liking for little Adele and Mrs. Fairfax. Isn't that so?"

"Yes, sir. In different ways I have an affection for both."

"Would you be sorry to part with them?" he inquired.

"Yes."

"It's a pity," he said, and sighed. "It is always the way of things in life. No sooner have you got settled in a pleasant place than you have to rise and move on."

"Must I move on, sir?" I asked. "Must I leave Thornfield?"

"I believe you must, Jane. I am sorry, Jane, but I believe you must indeed."

This was a blow, but I did not let it put me down. "Well, sir," I said, "I shall be ready when the order to march comes."

"It has come now. I must give it tonight."

"Are you going to be married, sir?"

"Exactly. You have hit the nail straight on the head."

"Soon, sir?"

"Very soon, Miss Eyre. I am not sure that my bride will be pleased to come into a household which includes a child and a governess. Adele must go to school. And you, Miss Eyre, must get a new position."

"Yes, sir, I will advertise immediately, and meantime I suppose—" I was going to say, "I suppose I may stay here till I find another place." But I stopped, for I was close to crying and my voice was not quite under my control.

"In about a month I hope to be a bridegroom," con-

tinued Mr. Rochester, "and in the meantime I shall myself look out for employment for you."

"Thank you, sir. I am sorry to give you the trouble."

"Oh, no need to apologize!" Mr. Rochester declared.
"I believe that when an employee does her duty as well
as you have done yours, she has a sort of claim upon
her employer for any little assistance he can conven-
iently give her. Indeed I have already heard of a place
that I think will suit. It is to act as governess for the
five daughters of Mrs. O'Gall of Bitternut Lodge in Con-
naught, Ireland."

"It is a long way off, sir."

"No matter—a girl of your sense will not object to
the voyage or the distance."

"I don't object to the voyage, but to the distance,"
said I. "And then the sea will separate me from—"

"From what, Jane?"

"From England and from Thornfield and—"

"Well?" he asked.

"From *you*, sir."

I said this almost without meaning to do so. At the
same time my tears gushed out. I did not cry so as to
let myself be heard by Mr. Rochester. I avoided sobbing
aloud. The thought of Mrs. O'Gall and Bitternut Lodge
struck cold to my heart. Even colder was the thought of
all the ocean brine and foam which would soon come
between me and the master at whose side I walked. But
coldest was the remembrance of the wider ocean of
wealth and position that came between me and the one
I naturally loved.

"It is a long way," I said again.

"It is, to be sure. When you get to Bitternut Lodge
in Ireland, Jane, I shall never see you again. That's certain. I never go over to Ireland. We have been good
friends, Jane, have we not?"

"Yes, sir."

"And when friends are about to part, they like to spend a little time together. Come—for half an hour or so we'll talk over the voyage and the parting quietly. Here is the chestnut tree. Here is the bench at its old roots. Come, we shall sit there in peace tonight, even though we shall never again sit there together." He seated me and himself.

"It is a long way to Ireland, Jane," he went on, "and I am sorry to send my little friend on such weary travels. But if I can't do better, how is it to be helped? When you have gone, will you forget me, Jane?"

"I shall never do that, sir. You know—" I broke off because it was impossible for me to continue. My heart was too full.

"Jane, do you hear that nightingale singing in the wood? Listen!"

In listening, I sobbed aloud. I could no longer hold back the sounds of my grief. When I did speak, it was only to wish that I had never been born, or never come to Thornfield.

"Because you are sorry to leave it?" asked Mr. Rochester.

"Yes, I am sorry to leave Thornfield. I love Thornfield. I love it because I have enjoyed living here. I have known you here, Mr. Rochester, and it fills me with sorrow to feel that I must be torn from you forever. I see the necessity of leaving, and it is like seeing the necessity of dying."

"Perhaps, after all, you need not go," he said suddenly.

"But what of Miss Ingram, your bride?"

"My bride! What bride? I have no bride."

"But you soon will have one."

"Yes, I will! I will!" He set his teeth.

"Then I must go, sir. You have said it yourself."

"No, you must stay! I swear it—and my oath shall be kept."

"I tell you I must go!" I replied with excitement. "Do you think I can stay to become nothing to you? Do you think I am a machine without feelings? Do you think that because I am poor, plain, and little, I am without a heart or soul? . . . You think wrong! I have as much heart and soul as you. And if God had given me some beauty and wealth, I should have made it as hard for you to leave me, as it now is for me to leave you."

"Don't speak that way!" exclaimed Mr. Rochester. He gathered me in his arms. "Don't speak that way, Jane."

"I must," I replied. "You are a married man—or as good as a married man, and wedded to a person who is beneath you. I do not believe you truly love Miss Ingram, for I have seen and heard you laugh at her ways. I would scorn such a marriage. Therefore, I am better than you, because I would not marry for wealth or beauty or high position. Let me go!"

"Where, Jane? To Ireland?"

"Yes—to Ireland. I have spoken my mind, and can go anywhere now."

"Jane, be still. Don't struggle so, as if you were a wild bird caught in a net."

"I am no bird, and no net holds me. I am a free human being with an independent will." With another effort I broke from his grasp and stood erect before him.

"And you shall independently decide your future," he said. "I offer you my hand, my heart, and a share of all my possessions."

"You are playing a game with me. Please don't amuse yourself at my expense."

"No," he declared, "I am asking you to pass through life at my side—to be my wife."

"For that fate," said I, "you have made your choice already, and must keep to it."

"Jane, be still a few moments. You are too much excited. I will be still too."

A breath of wind came sweeping down the walk and shook the boughs of the chestnut tree. Mr. Rochester sat quietly, looking at me gently and seriously. Some time passed before he spoke. At last he said, "Come to my side, Jane, and let us understand each other."

"I will never come to your side again. I am going away now and cannot return."

"But, Jane, I call you as my wife. It is you only I intend to marry."

I was silent. I thought he was jesting with me.

"Come, Jane—come here."

"Your bride stands between us."

He rose, and with a stride reached me.

"Here is my bride," he said, drawing me to him, "because here is my equal and my own kind. Jane, will you marry me?"

Still I did not answer, and still I tried to free myself from his grasp.

"Do you doubt me, Jane?"

"Entirely."

"Have you no faith in me?"

"Not a whit."

"Am I a liar in your eyes?" he asked angrily. "You *shall* be convinced. What love have I for Miss Ingram? None, and that you know. What love has she for me?

None, as I have taken pains to find out. I caused a rumor to reach her that my fortune was not a third of what she thought. After that I visited her to see the result. It was coldness both from her and her mother. I would not—I could not—marry Miss Ingram. It is you—poor and small and plain as you are—whom I beg to accept me as a husband."

"What, me!" I exclaimed, beginning to believe him. "Do you really want to marry me who have not a friend in the world except yourself—not a shilling but what you have given me?"

"Yes, Jane. I must have you for my own—entirely my own. Will you be mine? Say yes, quickly."

"Mr. Rochester, let me look at your face. Turn to the moonlight."

"Why?"

"Because I want to read your expression. Turn!"

"Oh, Jane, you torture me. With that searching look you torture me!" he exclaimed.

"Why," I asked, "did you take such pains to make me believe you wished to marry Miss Ingram?"

"Forgive me, Jane!" he said wildly. "It was a low trick! I meant to awaken your feelings through jealousy."

"Are you in earnest?" I questioned. "Do you sincerely wish me to be your wife?"

"I do. And if an oath is necessary to satisfy you, I swear it."

"Then, sir, I will marry you."

"Come to me—come to me entirely now," said he. In his deepest tone he spoke in my ear as he laid his cheek on mine, "Make my happiness, and I will make yours."

Before long he held me away from him at arm's length and asked, "Are you happy, Jane?"

"Yes," I replied. "Yes."

His next words were very strange. If I had learned their meaning then, my happiness would have been changed to sorrow in an instant. Turning his face toward the heavens, he spoke almost as if to himself. "I have found her friendless and comfortless. Now I shall guard and love and comfort her. The world may not approve of what I do, but surely the Almighty in His justice gives approval. As for man's opinion—I wash my hands of it."

Strange words from one who was about to become a bridegroom! I would have asked him what he meant, but a sudden change in the weather lost me the opportunity.

What had come upon the night? The moon had not yet set, but we were all in shadow. I could scarcely see my master's face, near as I was. And what ailed the chestnut tree? It twisted and groaned, while the wind roared and came sweeping over us. A flash of lightning leaped out of a cloud, and there was a crack, crash, and rattle of thunder. The rain rushed down.

"We must go in," said Mr. Rochester. "Sad thought! I could have sat with you till morning, Jane."

When I reached my room, I did not immediately go to sleep. I was full of happiness, and I wanted to tell someone of my joy that I was to be Mr. Rochester's bride. In this mood I sat down and wrote a letter telling the good news to my uncle in Madeira. Then I blew out my candle and crept beneath the covers.

It was a night when God's lightning crashed again and again upon the earth with peals of thunder. Before I left my bed in the morning, little Adele came running in to tell me that a bolt had struck the great horse-chestnut tree at the bottom of the orchard, and half of it had been split away.

12

The month of courtship had passed. Its very last hours were going quickly. There was no putting off the day that approached. The wedding day was to be tomorrow, and all preparations for its arrival were complete. I had nothing more to do. There were my trunks, packed, locked, and tied, and arranged in a row along the wall of my room. Tomorrow at this time they would be far on their road to London, and so should I. Only the address cards remained to be nailed on. Mr. Rochester had himself written on each card the address "Mrs. Rochester, Tower Hotel, London." I could not bring myself to attach them, or to have them attached. Mrs. Rochester did not exist. She would not be born till tomorrow, some time after eight o'clock in the morning. I would wait to be sure that she existed before I addressed all that property to her.

In the closet opposite my dressing table were my wedding gown and veil. It was nine o'clock, and at this evening hour the white garments shone dimly through the shadows. Shutting the door upon them, I said, "I will leave you by yourself, white dream. I am too nervous here and must go downstairs."

I had at heart a strange and anxious feeling. Something had happened which I could not understand. No one knew of the event except myself. It had taken place the previous night when Mr. Rochester had been away from home. Business had called him to a small estate of two or three farms which he owned. They were thirty miles off, and he had not yet returned. I waited for him now, eager to ask him whether he could solve the mystery that puzzled me.

I went to the library to discover whether the fire was lit. Though it was summer, the evening was gloomy, and I knew Mr. Rochester would like to see a cheerful hearth when he came in. Yes, the fire had been kindled for some time, and burnt well. I placed his armchair by the chimney corner, and I wheeled the table near it. I let down the curtain and had the candles brought in, ready for lighting. When I had completed these arrangements, I was more restless than ever. I could not sit still, nor even remain in the house. A little timepiece in the room and the old clock in the hall struck ten together.

"How late it grows!" I said. "I will run down to the gates. There is moonlight, and I can see a good way along the road. He may be coming now, and to meet him will save some minutes of suspense."

The wind roared high in the great trees which stood at the gates. As far as I could see, the road was still and deserted. A tear came into my eye while I looked; it was a tear of disappointment and impatience. During the time that I lingered, the night grew dark and rain came driving fast on the gale.

"I wish he would come! I wish he would come!" I exclaimed. I was seized by worry, for I had expected his arrival much earlier. What could be keeping him? Had an accident happened? The event of last night again came to my mind, and I felt it as a warning of trouble.

"Well, I cannot return to the house," I thought. "I cannot sit by the fireside while he is out in bad weather. I will go forward and meet him."

I walked fast, but not far. Before I had gone a

quarter of a mile, I heard the tramp of hoofs. A horseman came on, full speed, with a dog running at his side. It was Mr. Rochester mounted on Mesrour and followed by Pilot. Seeing me, he took off his hat and waved it around his head. I now ran to meet him.

"There!" he exclaimed, as he stretched out his hand and bent from the saddle. "You can't do without me. That is evident. Step on my boot-toe. Give me both hands. Mount!"

I obeyed, springing up on the horse before him. He gave me a warm welcome and paid me some pretty compliments, which I swallowed as well as I could. He checked himself in his gay greeting to demand, "But is there anything the matter, Jane, that you come to meet me at such an hour? Is there anything wrong?"

"I thought you never would come. I could not bear to wait in the house for you, especially with this rain and wind."

"Rain and wind, indeed! Yes, you are dripping. Pull my cloak round you. I think you are feverish, Jane. Both your cheek and hand are burning hot. I ask again, is there anything the matter?"

"Nothing, now that you are here. I am neither afraid nor unhappy now."

"Then you have been both before?"

"Yes, but I'll tell you all about it by-and-by, sir. And I suppose you will only laugh at me for my fears."

"I'll laugh at you heartily when tomorrow is past. Till then I dare not. My prize is not certain."

"Here we are at Thornfield. Now let me get down," said I.

He landed me on the pavement. As John took his horse and he followed me into the hall, he told me to hurry and join him in the library. In little more than five minutes I changed to dry things and came down, finding him at supper.

"Take a seat and keep me company, Jane. If all goes well, this is the next to the last meal you will eat at Thornfield Hall for a long time."

I sat down near him, but told him I could not eat.

"Is it because you have a journey before you, Jane? Is it the thought of going to London that takes away your appetite?"

"No, it is not that. Finish your supper first before we talk about it."

"Very well." Mr. Rochester hastened to eat his meal, and presently announced, "I have done, Jane."

I rang the servants' bell and ordered the tray to be taken away. When we were again alone, I stirred the fire and then took a low seat at my master's knee.

"It is near midnight," I said.

"Yes, Jane, but didn't you promise a few days ago that you would stay up with me the night before our wedding?"

"I did, and I will keep my promise for an hour or two at least. I have no wish to go to bed yet."

"Are all your arrangements complete?"

"All, sir."

"And so are mine," he returned. "I have settled everything. We leave Thornfield tomorrow within half an hour after our return from church."

"That's good, sir."

"With what a strange smile you said those words, Jane. Is anything wrong? Are you well?"

"I believe I am."

"Believe! What is the matter? Tell me what it is."

"Oh, sir! I wish this day would never end. Who knows what tomorrow may bring?"

"But tomorrow is to be our happy wedding day. You puzzle me, Jane. Your look and tone are mysterious. I want an explanation."

"Then, sir, listen. Something happened last night."

"Ah, I thought so from what you said before. It is probably nothing of importance, but it has disturbed you. Let me hear it. Has Mrs. Fairfax said something, perhaps? Or have you overheard the servants talking about you? It may be that your feelings have been hurt by jealous talk."

"No, sir, it is nothing like that. All day yesterday I was very busy and very happy in my preparations for our wedding. It was a fine day, if you remember. The calmness of the sky and air kept me from worrying about your safety and comfort on your journey. I walked a little while on the pavement after tea, but just at sunset the air turned cold and the sky cloudy. Therefore I went indoors. Sophie called me upstairs to look at my wedding dress, which had just been brought. Under it in the box I found a surprise gift. It was a veil of the most expensive material, which you had ordered from London. I thought how I would tease you about your trying to make your lowly bride masquerade in the costume of a high-born lady. I smiled at the thought of showing you the plain cloth I had already prepared— and I planned to ask you if it was not good enough for a woman who could bring her husband neither fortune, beauty, nor important relations."

"Of course your cloth was not good enough for my bride," interrupted Mr. Rochester. "But why are you so excited? What did you find in the veil besides its embroidery? Did you find poison or a dagger, that you look so unhappy now?"

"No, no, sir. Except for the richness of the fabric I

found nothing. But, sir, as it grew dark, the wind rose and blew wild and high with a moaning sound. I was glad to creep into bed and under the blankets. However, for some time I could not sleep. A feeling of anxious excitement upset me. I seemed to hear a mournful sound that was only partly lost in the noise of the rising wind. Whether the sound was in the house or outside I could not tell, but it was constantly repeated. At last I decided it must be some dog howling at a distance. On falling asleep, I continued to see in my dreams a dark and stormy night. I dreamt that you and I were out in the storm, walking on a highway. We came to a crossroads, and to my sorrow you went one way and I went the other. In my dream I wept because we were parting forever—yes, forever."

"And does the dream still trouble you now, Jane, when we are together? Well, you have been nervous! Forget this imaginary trouble and think only of real happiness!"

"I will try to forget it when I have finished my tale, but hear me to the end."

"But I thought, Jane, you had told me everything. I thought I had found the cause of your unhappy mood in a dream!"

I shook my head. "What!" he cried. "Is there more? But I will not believe it to be anything important. Go on."

"I have told you only the beginning, sir. The story is yet to come. I suddenly woke from my dream with a gleam of light dazzling my eyes. I thought that it must be daylight. But I was mistaken. It was only candlelight. Sophie, I supposed, must have come into my room. There was a light on my table, and the door of the closet, where I had hung my wedding dress and veil, stood open. Hearing a rustling noise in the closet, I asked, 'Sophie, what are you doing?' No one answered, but someone came out of the closet. This person took the light, held it up, and looked at the clothing in my traveling bag. 'Sophie! Sophie!' I again cried, but still there was no answer. Rising up in bed, I bent forward to look. First surprise and then amazement came over me. My blood crept cold through my veins! Mr. Rochester, it was not Sophie! It was not Leah! It was not Mrs. Fairfax! It was not even that strange woman, Grace Poole."

"It must have been one of them," interrupted my master.

"No, sir. I give you my word to the contrary. The shape standing before me had never been seen by me in Thornfield Hall till then. It was entirely new to me."

"Describe it, Jane."

"It seemed, sir, to be a woman who was fairly tall and had thick, dark hair hanging down her back. I could not make out what sort of dress she had on. It was white and straight, but whether it was a gown, sheet, or funeral robe I cannot say."

"Did you see her face?"

"Not at first. But presently she took my veil from its place. She held it up and gazed at it for a long time. Then she threw it over her head, and turned to the mirror. At that moment I saw the reflection of her face and features quite distinctly in the glass."

"What were they like?"

"Dreadful, sir. Oh, I never saw a face like it! It was a horrible face; it was a savage face. I wish I could forget the red eyes and the fearful, dark, and swollen features."

"Were they dark, Jane? Ghosts are usually pale."

"This one, sir, was purple. The lips were swelled

and dark. The forehead was wrinkled, and the black eyebrows were thick above the bloodshot eyes. Shall I tell you of what it reminded me?"

"You may."

"Of a vampire."

"Ah! What did it do?"

"Sir, it removed my veil from its head, tore it in two parts, threw them both on the floor, and stamped on them."

"Afterwards what happened?" asked Mr. Rochester.

"It pulled aside the window curtain and looked out. Perhaps it saw dawn approaching, for it took up the candle and started toward the door. Just at my bedside the figure stopped. She looked at me savagely, holding the candle close to my face. A great terror came over me, and I must have fainted."

"Who was with you when you revived?"

"No one, sir. It was broad daylight. I rose, bathed my head and face, and drank some water. I felt that, though weak from my fright, I was not ill. And I decided that I would tell this story to no one except you. Now, sir, tell me who and what that woman was."

"She was simply a dream," he said. "Of that I am certain. I must be careful of you, my treasure. Nerves like yours were not made for rough handling."

"Sir, depend on it that my nerves were not at fault. The thing was real. The happening actually took place."

"And your other dream? Was that real too? Have we been parted?" Mr. Rochester asked, smiling.

"Not yet," I replied.

"And are we about to be kept apart? Why, it is past midnight, and the day has already begun which is to see us married. Once we have been wedded, there shall be no return of these mental terrors."

"Mental terrors, sir! I wish I could believe them to be only in my imagination. I wish that more than ever now, since even you cannot explain to me the mystery of that awful visitor."

"And since I cannot explain it, Jane, it must have been unreal."

"Sir, I said to myself on awakening this morning. Then I looked round the room to gather courage and comfort from the cheerful appearance of each familiar object in full daylight. But there on the carpet I saw the proof that my midnight visitor had been real. On the floor I saw my veil, torn from top to bottom in two halves!"

I felt Mr. Rochester start and shudder. He hastily threw his arms around me. "Thank God!" he exclaimed. "If anything evil did come near you last night, it was only the veil that was harmed. Oh, to think what might have happened!"

For the first time he seemed really excited by my story. But in a few minutes he calmed himself and continued cheerily, "Now, Jane, I'll explain to you all about it. It was half dream and half real. I don't doubt that a woman did enter your room, and that woman must have been Grace Poole. You know what she tried to do to me —and what she succeeded in doing to Mason! While you were half-awake and half-asleep, you witnessed her actions in your room. Being nervous and excited, you imagined that she had a strange ghostlike appearance, different from her own. Of course, the spiteful tearing of the veil was real, and it is like her to do such a thing. I know you wonder why I keep such a woman in my house. When we have been married a year and a day, I will tell you, but not now. Are you satisfied, Jane? Do you accept my solution of the mystery?"

I thought it over, and in truth it appeared to me the only possible explanation. I was not entirely satisfied, but to please him I tried to appear so. I certainly did feel relieved, so I answered him with a contented smile. And now, as it was long past one, I prepared to leave him.

"Doesn't Sophie sleep with Adele in the nursery?" he asked, as I lit my candle.

"Yes, sir."

"And there is room enough in Adele's little bed for you. You must share it with her tonight, Jane. After such an experience as you have had, it is no wonder that you are nervous. I would prefer that you do not remain alone. Promise me to go to the nursery."

"I shall be very glad to do so, sir."

"And lock the door carefully on the inside. Wake Sophie when you go upstairs and tell her to get you up early tomorrow, for you must be dressed and have finished breakfast before eight. And now, no more black thoughts. Chase trouble and care away, Jane. Don't you hear how the wind and rain have quieted? Look here— it is a lovely night." He lifted up the curtain for me to see.

It was as he said. The clouds were being driven away by a light wind. The moon shone peacefully.

"Well," said Mr. Rochester, gazing questioningly into my eyes, "how is my little Jane now?"

"The night is calm, sir, and so am I."

13

Sophie came at seven to help me dress. We were very long at this task. Indeed, we were so long that Mr. Rochester, impatient at my delay, sent up to ask why I did not come. Sophie was just arranging my hair, and we hurried to finish as soon as we could. Between us we put on the veil that I had made and fastened it to my hair with a brooch.

As I hastened to the door, Sophie cried in French, "Stop! Look at yourself in the mirror."

I turned and saw in the glass a robed and veiled figure. It was so different from my usual self that it seemed almost the image of a stranger. "Jane!" called Mr. Rochester. At the sound of his impatient voice I went hurriedly out of the room and down the stairs, at the foot of which I was received by my bridegroom.

"Tardy one!" he exclaimed. "I am on fire with impatience, and you are delaying so long!"

He took me into the dining room, looked me over keenly, and declared me "fair as a lily, and not only the pride of his life, but the desire of his eyes." Then, telling me that he would give me but ten minutes to eat some breakfast, he rang the bell. One of the servants answered it.

"Is John getting the carriage ready?"

"Yes, sir."

"Is the luggage being brought down?"

"They are bringing it down now, sir."

"Go to the church. See whether the clerk and the

priest, Mr. Wood, are there. Then return and tell me."

The church was only just beyond the gates, and the footman was back in a short time.

"Mr. Wood is ready, sir," he said.

"And the carriage?" asked Mr. Rochester.

"The horses are being harnessed."

"We shall not want it to go to church," said the master, "but it must be ready the moment we return. Have all the boxes and luggage arranged and strapped on. See that the coachman is in his seat. We shall be off for London immediately after the wedding."

"Yes, sir."

"Jane, are you ready?"

I rose. There were no bridesmaids, no groomsmen, no relatives to wait for—none but Mr. Rochester and me. Mrs. Fairfax stood in the hall as we passed. I would have spoken to her, but my hand was held in a grasp of iron. I was hurried along so that I could hardly follow. To look at Mr. Rochester was to feel that not a second of delay would be allowed for any purpose. I wonder what other bridegroom ever looked as he did—sternly determined and with flaming, flashing eyes.

At the churchyard gate he stopped. He discovered I was quite out of breath. "Am I cruel to you in my impatience?" he said. "Stop for a minute. Lean on me, Jane."

I can recall the gray old church as it looked that morning. I remember, too, something of the green graves nearby. I have not forgotten, either, the two strangers who were walking about in the graveyard. I noticed them because, as they saw us, they passed around to the back of the church. I did not doubt that they were going to enter by the side door and watch the wedding. Mr. Rochester did not see them, for he was earnestly looking at my face.

We entered the quiet and humble temple. The priest was waiting at the altar with the clerk beside him. All was still except for two shadowy figures that moved in a far corner. My guess had been correct. The strangers had slipped in before us, and they now stood in the rear with their backs toward us.

We took our place at the altar. Hearing a quiet step behind me, I glanced over my shoulder. One of the strangers was advancing up the aisle.

The service began. When the priest had finished with the first part, he came a step forward and said, "I now ask you both that if either of you know any reason why you may not be lawfully joined together in marraige, you now confess it."

It is the custom for the priest to stop a moment at this point as if waiting for a reply. However, it is only a custom, and certainly he expected no answer. He remained silent only for a moment. Then he stretched his hand toward Mr. Rochester, as he prepared to ask, "Will you have this woman for your wedded wife?"

At that instant a clear voice said, "The marriage cannot go on. I declare that this man and woman cannot be lawfully wedded."

The priest looked up at the speaker and stood as if he had been struck dumb. The clerk did the same. Mr. Rochester moved unsteadily, as if an earthquake had rolled under his feet. Taking a firmer footing, and not turning his head or eyes, he said, "Continue."

Silence fell when he had uttered that word. Presently Mr. Wood said, "I cannot continue without some investigation into what has been said. I must have proof of its truth or falsehood."

"This wedding must be stopped," declared the voice behind us. "I am in a position to prove what I say. It is unlawful for this man and woman to wed."

Mr. Rochester heard this, but said nothing. He stood stiff and stubborn, making no movement, except to grasp my hand. How like marble was his pale, firm, strong expression at this moment! How his eyes shone, watchful and yet wild!

Mr. Wood seemed hardly to know what to do. "What is the reason that this wedding is unlawful?" he asked. "Perhaps it may be explained away."

"Hardly," was the answer. "I have called it unlawful, and I know what I am talking about." The speaker came forward and leaned on the rail. He continued to speak, uttering each word distinctly and calmly.

"The reason is a former marriage. Mr. Rochester has a wife now living."

My nerves jumped at those quiet words as they had never jumped at thunder. My blood ran both cold and hot as it had never run for frost or fire, but I was steady enough to be in no danger of fainting. I looked at Mr. Rochester, and I made him look at me. His whole face was hard as rock. His eyes seemed filled with sparks. He denied nothing. Without speaking and without smiling he only clasped my waist with his arm and held me to his side.

"Who are you?" he asked the stranger.

"My name is Briggs. I am a lawyer of Wick Street, London."

"Do you claim that I have a wife?"

"I remind you that she still lives, sir. And that the law considers her your wife, even if you do not."

"Tell me her name, her parents' names, and her address," ordered my bridegroom.

"Certainly. I have here a paper which contains the facts, and they are all sworn to by a gentleman who knows the truth of the matter as well as I know my own name. Let me read what he says." Mr. Briggs calmly took the paper from his pocket and read aloud: "I swear and can prove that Edward Fairfax Rochester of Thornfield Hall, England, was married to my sister, Bertha Antoinetta Mason, in the church at Spanish Town, Jamaica. The record of the marriage will be found in that church. A copy of it is now in my possession. Signed, *Richard Mason.*"

The lawyer replaced the paper in his pocket.

"That may prove I have been married," said Mr. Rochester, "but it does not prove that the woman mentioned as my wife is still living."

"She was still living three months ago," returned the lawyer.

"How do you know?"

"I have a witness to the fact, sir."

"Produce him—or go to blazes."

"I will produce him. He is right here. Mr. Mason, have the goodness to step forward."

On hearing that name, Mr. Rochester set his teeth. Being close to him, I felt a shudder of either anger or hopelessness run through his body.

The second stranger, who had remained in the rear, now came forward. A pale face looked over the lawyer's shoulder. Yes, it was Mason himself. Mr. Rochester turned and glared at him. He lifted his strong arm. With a blow, he could have struck Mason and dashed the breath from his body, but the man drew away and cried, "Don't, Fairfax!"

Then Mr. Rochester's anger cooled. He only asked, "What have *you* to say?"

The reply stuck on Mason's lips.

"The devil is in it if you cannot answer!" cried the bridegroom. "I again demand, what have *you* to say?"

"Sir—sir," interrupted the priest. "Do not forget you are in a sacred place." Then speaking to Mason, he inquired gently, "Do you know, sir, whether or not this gentleman's wife is still living?"

"Have courage, Mason," urged the lawyer. "Speak out."

"She is now living at Thornfield Hall," said Mason. "I saw her there last April. I am her brother."

"At Thornfield Hall!" exclaimed the priest. "Impossible! I have lived long in the neighborhood, sir, and I never heard of a Mrs. Rochester at Thornfield Hall."

I saw a grim smile twist Mr. Rochester's lip, and he muttered, "No! I took care that none should hear of it. No one knows her as Mrs. Rochester. But, enough! Everything shall be told now. Wood, close your book and take off your robe. Clerk Green, leave the church. There will be no wedding today. Gentlemen, my plan is broken up! What this lawyer and his client say is true. I have been married, and the woman to whom I was married still lives! Wood, you say you never heard of a Mrs. Rochester at my house, but surely you must have heard about the mysterious lunatic kept there under lock and key. I now inform you that she is my wife, whom I married some years ago. Bertha Mason was the name of my bride, and she is the sister of this brave person who stands here with his shivering limbs and white cheeks. Cheer up, Dick! Never fear me! I'd just as soon strike a woman as you. Bertha Mason is insane, and she came from a family that had a long history of madness. Her mother was both a mad woman and a drunkard! I found that out *after* I had married the daughter, for they were silent about family secrets before. After our marriage, Bertha turned into a lunatic and drunkard like her mother. Oh, my life has been horrible, if you only knew it! But I owe you no further explanation. Briggs, Wood, Mason—I invite you all to come up to the house and visit *my wife!* You shall see what sort of a being I was cheated into marrying. You shall judge whether or not I had a right to forget this woman who is no longer a wife to me and to seek one who could really be my true partner in marriage."

Mr. Rochester pointed at me and continued, "This girl knew no more of the disgusting secret than you did, Wood. She thought all was fair and lawful, and never dreamt she was being trapped into marrying a miserable man already tied to a mad woman! Come, all of you! Follow me."

Still holding me fast, he left the church. The three gentlemen came after us. At the front door of the Hall we found the carriage.

"Take it back to the coach house, John," said Mr. Rochester coolly. "It will not be wanted today."

When we entered the house, Mrs. Fairfax, Adele, Sophie, and Leah advanced to meet and greet us.

"Face right about, everyone!" cried the master. "Away with your congratulations! Who wants them?— Not I! They are too late for *my* wedding!"

He passed on up the stairs, still holding my hand. He motioned the gentlemen to follow him, and they did. We mounted the first staircase, passed up the corridor, and proceeded to the third story. The low, black door was opened by Mr. Rochester's key.

"You know this place, Mason," said the master. "She bit and stabbed you here."

He lifted the tapestry hangings from the wall, uncovering the second door. This, too, he opened. Inside was a room without a window. It was lighted by a fire and by a lamp hanging from the ceiling by a chain.

Grace Poole bent over the fire, cooking something in a saucepan. At the far end of the room a figure ran backwards and forwards. Whether it was beast or human being, one could not tell at first sight. It was crawling on its hands and knees. It growled like some strange wild animal, but it was covered with clothing. Hair that was as wild as a horse's mane hid its head and face.

"Good day, Nurse Poole!" said Mr. Rochester. "How are you? And how is your patient today?"

"She's fair, sir, I thank you," replied Grace as she lifted the boiling pan off the fire. "She's rather snappish, but not too wild."

At that moment a savage cry made us doubt her favorable report. The beast rose up and stood tall on her feet.

"Ah, sir, she sees you!" exclaimed Grace. "You'd better not stay."

"Only a few moments, Grace. You must allow me a few moments."

"Take care then, sir! For goodness' sake, take care!"

The lunatic roared loudly. She parted her hair away from her face and gazed wildly at her visitors. I recognized well that purple face and those swollen features. Mrs. Poole stood in front of her to prevent her from rushing at us.

"Keep out of the way," said Mr. Rochester, pushing Grace aside. "She has no knife, now, I suppose? Besides, I'm on my guard."

"One never knows if she has one or not, sir. She is so cunning."

"We had better leave her," whispered Mason.

"Go to the devil!" was his brother-in-law's reply.

"Watch out!" cried Grace. The three gentlemen stepped back. Mr. Rochester put me behind him. The lunatic sprang forward, seized his throat, and set her teeth in his cheek. They struggled with one another. She was a big woman, almost as tall as her husband and heavily built besides. She showed a man's strength in the contest. More than once she almost choked him, athletic as he was. He could have settled her with one blow. But he would not strike. He would only wrestle. At last he mastered her arms and tied them behind her with a cord Grace Poole gave him. With more rope he bound her to a chair. Mr. Rochester then turned to the others. He looked at them with a smile both sad and bitter.

"That is *my wife*," said he. Laying his hand on my shoulder, he continued, "and this is the woman I wished to have. Wood and Briggs, look at the difference! Compare these clear eyes with the red ones over there. Compare this face with that one. Then judge if I was wrong in what I tried to do today! Out with you now! I must lock the door upon this precious jewel of a wife."

We all went out. Mr. Rochester stayed a moment behind us to give some further orders to Grace Poole. The lawyer spoke to me as he walked down the stair.

"You, madam," said he, "are cleared from all blame. Your uncle will be glad to hear it. That is, he will be glad to hear it if he is still alive."

"My uncle!" I cried. "What of him? Do you know him?"

"Mr. Mason does," replied the lawyer. "Your uncle, John Eyre, for some years has been the Madeira representative of the company with which Mr. Mason is connected. Mr. Mason happened to be stopping over in Madeira on his way home to Jamaica when Mr. Eyre received your letter about your coming marriage. Knowing that Mr. Mason was acquainted with a gentleman by the name of Rochester, your uncle mentioned this news to him. Mr. Mason at once declared that it was impossible. He informed your uncle that Mr. Rochester already had a wife. Upon hearing that information, John Eyre begged Mr. Mason to return to England and stop the wedding. Unfortunately, your unhappy relative could not come himself because he lay on a sick bed, suffering from an illness that cannot be cured. Therefore he asked Mason to take care of the matter. On his way here Mr. Mason stopped at my office in London and asked me to come with him to Thornfield Hall. I am thankful indeed that we were not too late. If I were not certain that your uncle will be dead before you can reach him, I should advise you to go to him. As it is, I think you had better remain in England. Well, that is all I can tell you. Have we anything else to stay for?" he asked, turning to Mason.

"No, no—let us be gone," was the anxious reply. Without waiting to take leave of Mr. Rochester, they made their exit at the hall door. The priest stayed to say a few words to Mr. Rochester, and then he too left.

When the others had gone, I shut myself in my room. Sadly, I took off the wedding dress and put on the gown I had worn the day before. I then sat down, feeling weak and tired. I leaned my arms on a table, and my head dropped on them. All my hopes were dead.

14

Sometime in the afternoon I unlocked the door of my bedroom and stepped out into the corridor. I found Mr. Rochester sitting in a chair just outside my room.

"You have come out at last," he said. "Well, I have been waiting for you a long time. Although I have been listening carefully, I have not heard a single sound. In another five minutes I should have forced the lock like a burglar. Why do you shut yourself up alone? I see no trace of tears upon your cheek. No doubt you have been crying inside you. No doubt your heart has been weeping tears of blood. Jane, I never meant to hurt you so. Will you ever forgive me?"

I forgave him at that moment and on that spot. There was such deep regret in his eye, such true sorrow in his tone, and such great love in his whole look that I forgave him completely. Yet I could not tell him so in words, for my heart was too full of pain.

"You think I have treated you badly, Jane, don't you?" he asked.

"Yes, sir."

"Then tell me so. Don't spare me."

"I cannot. I am tired and sick. I want some water."

Taking me tenderly in his arms, he carried me downstairs to the library. Although it was summer, I shivered as if with cold. Mr. Rochester built a fire, and its warmth felt good. Then he put wine to my lips and gave me something to eat. Soon I began to feel more like myself.

"How are you now, Jane?"

"Much better, sir."

Standing before me, Mr. Rochester looked at me closely. Then he sat down beside me. "Will you listen to me?" he asked.

"Yes, for hours if you wish."

"Jane, did you ever hear that I was not the eldest son in my family? Did you know that I once had a brother older than I?"

"I remember that Mrs. Fairfax told me once."

"And did you ever hear that my father was a man who thought of little besides money? He was anxious always to have people respect him for his wealth, and he cared nothing whether they thought him a good, kind, or worthy man."

"I have heard something about that," I said.

"Well, Jane, my father decided that when he died, he would leave all his property to my brother Rowland. If divided in two, the Rochester fortune would not seem so great or important. Still, he could not bear the thought that a son of his should be a poor man. Therefore he looked for a wealthy woman whom I might marry. He found what he wanted in the daughter of an old acquaintance, Mr. Mason, who was a planter and merchant in the West Indies. When I left college, I was sent off to visit the Masons."

"Did you know that your father intended you to marry Mr. Mason's daughter for her wealth?" I asked.

"I knew only that my father considered Miss Mason a good match. He said nothing about her money, but told me that she was the boast and toast of Spanish Town for her beauty. Being young and foolish then, I thought that beauty was the most important quality in a woman or a wife."

"Have you changed your opinion on that subject, sir?"

"I have, indeed," declared Mr. Rochester. "I know now that it is the least important. I have learned to place the highest value on what is in her heart and mind. I have learned to love you, Jane, for the goodness of your character. But, to return to my story, I found that my father had not lied. Bertha Mason was a fine woman, in the style of Blanche Ingram—tall, dark, and queenly. Her father and brother wished me to marry her because I was from a good family; and so did she. They let me see her at parties. I was seldom with her alone and had very little private conversation with her. Everything went in such a way as to push me into marriage. Her charms dazzled me. Other young men who were my rivals awoke my jealousy and made me determined to win her. Her relatives encouraged me. I was swept off my feet, so that I married this woman whom I hardly knew at all."

"But surely," I cried, "even if you knew very little about her, you would have noticed if she had then been anything like the poor creature locked upstairs."

My sad master shook his head with a sigh. "At the time of our wedding she was sane enough. But what I did not know was that insanity ran in her family. My bride's mother I had never seen. I believed she was dead. When the honeymoon was over, I learned my mistake. The mother was mad, and shut up in a lunatic asylum. With her was another brother who was also insane. My father and my brother Rowland knew all this. However, they thought only of the Mason fortune and joined in the plot to have me marry Bertha."

"And how was it after you married her?" I inquired.

"Jane, I will not trouble you with all the detestable

details. I found that she and I were hopelessly unsuited to one another. Her tastes were entirely different from my own. I could not pass a single hour of the day with her in comfort. We could not converse together because we were not interested in the same things. She had a violent temper and would often burst into a wild rage. No servant, therefore, was willing to stay with us long. What is worse, she began to drink a great deal of liquor and to engage in all kinds of wickedness."

"I know it is a terrible thing to do, but could not your marriage have been legally ended?"

"Ah, just when I was coming to the idea, the doctors discovered that my wife was mad. Her drinking and evil habits had driven her into insanity. Jane, you don't like my story. You look almost sick. Shall I omit the rest?"

"No, sir, proceed. What did you do when you found she was mad?"

"After the doctors declared her mad, she was locked up in the house. One night I was awakened by her yells. My ears were filled by the curses shrieked out by the lunatic. I decided that to live this way was to live in hell. I kneeled down and unlocked a trunk which contained a pair of loaded pistols. I meant to shoot myself. But that intention quickly passed away. A breeze from the ocean blew in my window, and I thought to myself, 'Why not go back across the sea to the shores from which that wind blows? If I could not find worthwhile happiness there, I might at least enjoy a few worthless pleasures. In Europe no one would know that I was married to this horrible creature.' During those four years that I had lived in the West Indies, conditions at home had changed. My father and brother were dead, and I was master of Thornfield Hall and of the Rochester fortune. It is lucky that, because they feared my marriage might not turn out well, they had never told our friends about it. I could lock up my mad wife in Thornfield Hall and travel in Europe for my pleasure."

Unhappy memories were written on Mr. Rochester's face.

"Did everything go as you expected?"

"Yes, I took her to England, and it was a terrible voyage with such a monster. I was glad when I saw her safely shut in that third-story room which she has turned into a wild beast's den for the past ten years. I had some trouble to find someone to attend her, as it was necessary to select a person who would faithfully keep my secret. Bertha's ravings were bound to betray the fact that she was my wife to whoever took care of her. At last, I hired Grace Poole. She and Doctor Carter are the only ones to whom I admitted the whole truth. Mrs. Fairfax may indeed have suspected something, but she could never have learned all the facts exactly. On the whole, Grace has proved a good keeper, except for a few unfortunate occasions when she has been caught off guard. The lunatic is both cunning and vicious. She has never failed to take advantage of her guardian's slips. Once she stole a knife in order to stab her brother. Another time she managed to get the key to her door, and letting herself out, tried to burn me in my bed. On another night she paid that dreadful visit to you. How thankful I am that her fury was spent only on your wedding apparel! Ah, when I think how you might have been hurt, my blood curdles—"

"Don't talk any more of those days, sir." I interrupted, dashing some tears away from my eyes.

"No, Jane," he replied. "What is the use of thinking about the past when the future is so much brighter? I shall be happy as long as I have you by my side."

A sob broke from my lips, expressing all my sorrow for him and for myself. "Mr. Rochester, while you have a wife, I cannot remain by your side."

"Jane, do you mean to go one way in the world, and allow me to go another?"

"I do."

He bent towards me and took me in his arms. "Jane, do you mean it now?" I made no reply.

He softly kissed my forehead and cheek. "And now?" he asked.

"I do," I replied, pulling myself away from his embrace.

"You are going, Jane?"

"I am going, sir."

"You will not stay to comfort me? My deep love is nothing to you?"

"Indeed it is!" I cried. "But I must leave."

He turned his face away, and I got up and walked across the room. "Oh, Jane! my hope—my love—my life!" he exclaimed in a voice full of pain.

I had already reached the door, but I turned back. I walked back and knelt by his side. I turned his face toward me. I kissed his cheek. I smoothed his hair with my hand.

"God bless you, my dear master!" I said. "May you be kept from harm and wrong. May you be rewarded well for your past kindness to me." Then I stood up and at once went out of the room.

That night I never expected to sleep, but slumber fell on me nevertheless. Bad dreams tortured me, and I tossed and turned. After one frightful nightmare I awoke to find that it was just before dawn. "It cannot be too early to begin what I have to do," thought I. When I rose, I was already dressed, for I had taken off nothing but my shoes. I gathered up some clothing and other articles. In seeking these, I came across a pearl necklace which Mr. Rochester had forced me to accept on our wedding morning. I left that, because I did not feel it was mine. It belonged to the bride who had melted into thin air. The other articles I made into a parcel. My purse, containing twenty shillings, I put into my pocket. I slipped on my straw bonnet and pinned my shawl. In addition to my parcel, I carried my shoes in my hand, for I was anxious to make no noise. Silently, I stole from my room.

"Farewell, kind Mrs. Fairfax!" I whispered as I glided past her door. "Farewell, my darling Adele!" I said as I glanced towards the nursery. I did not dare to go in and look at her once more while she slept in her little bed. I could not risk being detected by the fine ear of Mr. Rochester, who, for all I knew, might be listening.

Somehow I could not get past Mr. Rochester's door without pausing. My heart seemed to skip a beat, and my foot was forced to stop also. Mr. Rochester was not asleep. I could hear him walking restlessly from wall to wall. Again and again he sighed while I listened.

Drearily, I wound my way downstairs. I knew what I had to do, and I did it mechanically. I searched in the kitchen for the key of the side door. I searched and found, too, a bottle of oil with which I oiled the key and lock. I got some water and some bread, for perhaps I should have to walk far. All this I did without one sound. I opened the door, passed out, and shut it softly. Dim dawn glimmered in the yard. As I passed through the gates, I turned to look at the house once again. Then I walked on down the road. Two great tears were trickling down my cheeks.

"Farewell!" was the cry of my heart. Despair added, "Farewell, forever!"

15

Five weeks had passed, and I was far from Thornfield Hall. Through the help of the parson in the little country village of Morton I had found a position as the teacher in a tiny school for girls. My situation as schoolmistress was a humble one. The pupils were poor. The cost of their education, including my own salary of thirty pounds a year, was paid by the only rich man in that part of the country. This kind man, Mr. Oliver, was the owner of a needle factory and an iron foundry, which furnished work for nearly all in the vicinity who were not farmers.

The name by which I called myself was Jane Elliot, and so I was known to the people of Morton. Because I was anxious to cut myself off from the friends I had known in the past, I did not use my true name. In this way I hoped to avoid being traced.

My home was a cottage, which downstairs consisted of a single room with whitewashed walls and a rough floor. It contained four painted chairs and a table, a clock, a cupboard with a few plates and dishes, a stove, and a set of tea things. Upstairs was a room of about the same size as the one below. In addition to the bed in this chamber, there was a chest of drawers, which, small as it seemed, was still too large to be filled by my few articles of clothing.

It was evening. I had sent home the little orphan who sometimes helped me put my tiny house in order. I was sitting alone before the fireplace, thinking. That

144

morning the village school had opened. I had twenty pupils. They spoke with such a strange country accent that they and I had difficulty in understanding one another. Some were rough. Others were gentle. All were ignorant, but wished to learn. It was my duty to remember that these daughters of poor, hard-working parents were of flesh and blood as good as any children of the richest families. I felt proud to be a schoolteacher with so much opportunity to help others, and it took away some of my sadness at having left Thornfield Hall.

Interrupting my thoughts at this point, I rose and went to my door. Outside, the sun was setting and the birds were singing their last songs of the day. As I looked at the scene, I thought myself almost happy, but suddenly I was surprised to find myself weeping. "Why am I crying?" I thought. "It is because I am lonely for Mr. Rochester—for him whom I shall never see again."

At this thought I turned my face aside from the lovely evening sky. I hid my eyes and leaned my head against the stone frame of my door. Soon, however, a slight noise near the garden gate made me look up. A dog was pushing the gate with his nose. I recognized him as Carlo, the pet of Mr. St. John Rivers, parson of our little village. It was this man who had helped me when I had first come to Morton. A penniless and hungry wanderer, I had got off the coach at this strange place after my flight from Thornfield. It had been as far as I was able to go on the fare I could pay. Not knowing how else to get food and work and a roof over my head, I had then gone to seek aid from the minister of the village. He had proved to be a kind, helpful young gentleman and had solved all my problems.

Now here he was at my gate, having appeared a minute or two after his dog. Mr. Rivers leaned upon the

wooden slats with his folded arms. His serious gaze was fixed on me. I asked him to come in.

"No," he replied. "I cannot stay. I have only brought you a little parcel of things you may need. It contains a box of watercolors, pencils, and paper."

I approached to take it. As I did so, I thought what a kind and welcome gift it was. He looked at my face closely as I came near him. Doubtless, he could see the traces of tears upon it.

"Have you found your first day's work harder than you expected?" he asked.

"Oh, no! On the contrary, I think that I shall get on with my pupils very well."

"Then perhaps you have been disappointed by the cottage and its furniture? They are, in truth, poor enough, but—"

I interrupted him quickly, saying, "My cottage is clean and weatherproof. My furniture is more than sufficient. All these things make me very thankful. If there is anything I lack, it is not a carpet or a sofa or silver plate. Besides, a few weeks ago I had nothing and came to you as a beggar. Now I have acquaintances, a home, and work. What reason have I to be unhappy?"

"Very well," said St. John Rivers. "I hope you really feel as contented as you say. You have told me nothing about your past life, and I do not wish to know your secrets. However, I should advise you not to look back on what is done. Look into the future, not the past."

"That is what I mean to do," I answered.

"You know," he continued, "a year ago I was myself very unhappy. I thought I had made a mistake by becoming a minister. I was bored to death by my quiet life. I was on fire to be anything rather than a priest. Why, thought I, hadn't I become something more exciting? A soldier, or anything else full of action and excitement. At first I did nothing but pity myself and feel miserable. Then I began to think how to solve my problem. At last I hit upon it. There is work I can do which requires all the qualifications of soldier, orator, statesman, and minister. It is to be a missionary, and that is what I have decided to become. What is more, from the moment I made up my mind on how to take care of my future, I have felt very happy. I know now exactly what I am going to do. As soon as someone can be found to take my place in Morton, I shall be off for India to take up my duties as a missionary. It is much better, Miss Elliot, to plan a happy future than to look back at a sad past."

When St. John Rivers finished speaking, both of us were silent for a moment, watching the last rays of the setting sun. We had our backs to the path and heard no sound on its grassy track. It was enough to startle us, therefore, when from behind us a gay voice, sweet as a silver bell, exclaimed, "Good evening, Mr. Rivers. And good evening, old Carlo. Your dog is quicker to recognize his friends than you are, sir. He pricked up his ears and wagged his tail when I was still at the bottom of the hill."

Now it happened that I had had a good view of Mr. River's face when the first sound of the speaker's voice fell upon his ears. I saw a rush of blood turn his cheeks red. I saw his eyes fill with fire. His chest expanded with a mighty breath. It was clear to me that St. John Rivers had a deep interest in this lovely young lady.

She was a perfect beauty. Her features were delicate. Her eyes were shaped and colored as we see them in pictures—large and dark and full. Her eyelashes were long and shadowy. Her eyebrows were as thin as if they had been drawn with a pencil. Her forehead was smooth and without lines. Her cheek was soft and fresh. Her lips were red and sweetly formed. Such even and gleaming teeth she had! Such an attractive dimple on her chin! Such rich, shining hair! All the advantages of beauty were hers. I admired her with my whole heart.

How did St. John Rivers act toward this angel? He acted as if her presence meant nothing to him at all. After one short glance at her he turned his eyes toward a cluster of daisies near his feet.

"A lovely evening, but late for you to be out alone," he said, kicking at the flowers with his foot.

"Oh, I just came home from Stokes. Papa told me you had opened your school, and that the new mistress had come. So I put on my bonnet after tea, and ran up the valley to see her. Is this lady the new teacher?" she asked, pointing to me.

"She is," said St. John.

"Do you think you shall like Morton?" she asked in a sweet, childish voice.

"I hope I shall. I have many reasons to do so."

"Did you find your pupils as attentive as you expected?" she inquired.

"Quite."

"Do you like your house?"

"Very much."

"I was the one who furnished it," she told me proudly. "Do you think it was done nicely?"

"Very nicely, indeed."

"And did I make a good choice in the girl who helps you?"

"You did, indeed." After I said these words, both she and I fell silent and looked each other up and down, as women have a way of doing. So, I thought, this is

Miss Oliver, the rich manufacturer's daughter. She is the one whose father pays my salary. How lucky she is in having been born both rich and beautiful!

"I shall come up to help you teach sometimes," she continued. "It will be a change for me to visit you now and then, and I like a change, for it is so dull in Morton. Mr. Rivers, I have been *so* gay during my stay at Stokes. Last night—or rather this morning—I was dancing till two o'clock. The Seventh Regiment is stationed there, and the officers are the sweetest men in the world. They put all the young fellows in Morton to shame."

It seemed to me that St. John's lips turned down at the corners as if he did not like this. However, his whole expression remained cold and stern.

As he stood, silent and serious, she leaned over to pet Carlo. "Poor Carlo loves me," said she. "*He* is not stern and chilly to his friends, and if he could speak, he would not be silent."

Watching St. John, I could see that he was only pretending to be cool toward Miss Oliver. But why he should do so, I could not yet understand.

Since he made no reply, she continued, "You are quite a stranger at Vale Hall. Papa complains that you never come to see us now. He is alone this evening, and not very well. Will you return with me and visit him?"

"It is too late in the day to call on Mr. Oliver," answered St. John.

"Too late! But, I declare, it is not. It is just the hour when Papa most wants company. The works are closed, and he has no business to occupy him. Now, Mr. Rivers, *do* come. Why are you so very shy? Do come and see Papa."

"Not tonight, Miss Rosamond, not tonight."

"Well, if you are so obstinate, I will leave you. Good evening!"

She held out her hand, and he just barely touched it. "Good evening," he repeated in a low voice. She started to move away, but then turned back.

"Are you well?" she asked. The question was a reasonable one, for his face was as pale as her gown.

"Quite well," he responded, and with a bow he left the gate. She went one way, and he another. She turned twice to gaze after him, but he walked on rapidly and never turned at all.

"Now that is strange," said I to myself. "Unless I am wrong, St. John Rivers loves Miss Oliver. Yet no matter how much he suffers, he refuses to give her any sign of his feelings. What can be his reason?" And puzzling over this problem, I almost began to forget my own troubles.

16

I continued the work of the village school as faithfully as I could. It was truly hard at first. Some time passed before I came to know my pupils. Many showed themselves obliging, and friendly, too. I discovered among them quite a few who were naturally polite and of excellent ability, so that they won my good will and admiration. They soon took a pleasure in doing their work well, in keeping themselves neat, and in learning quiet and orderly manners. I had among my students several farmers' daughters, who were almost grown women. These could already read, write, and sew; and to them I taught geography, history, and the finer kinds of needlework. I began to like the girls, and they liked me. Their parents loaded me with simple gifts. I became a favorite in the neighborhood.

Rosamond Oliver kept her word in coming to visit me. Her call at the school was generally made in the course of her morning ride. She would canter up to the door on her pony, followed by a mounted servant. Anything more perfect than her appearance in her purple riding habit, with her black velvet cap placed gracefully above the long curls that floated to her shoulders, can scarcely be imagined. She generally came at the hour when Mr. Rivers was giving a short daily lesson. When she went up and spoke to him, his hands would tremble and his eyes would burn. But he did nothing else to encourage her.

Miss Oliver also paid frequent visits to my cottage. I came to know her very well. Although she had always had everything she wanted, she was not spoiled. While she glanced at herself often in my looking glass, it was no more than any woman would have done. She was not over-conceited. She was always gay and lively. There was nothing serious or thoughtful about her.

One evening in her usual childish way she went poking about curiously into the nooks and corners of my house. Before long she discovered my drawing materials and some sketches. At first she was surprised, then delighted.

"Did you do these pictures?" she cried. "What a love—what a miracle you are! You draw better than my teacher in the school at Stokes. Will you draw a sketch of me to show to Papa?"

"With pleasure," I replied. I felt a thrill of delight at the thought of the beautiful picture it would be. Taking out a sheet of cardboard, I drew a careful outline. After some time I found that it was growing too late to continue working, and we stopped for the evening.

On each of the next few days Rosamond came to sit for her picture. It went along steadily, and at last I told her that I could finish the final touches without her. So it was that on the fifth of November, which was a school holiday, I was alone in my little house and hard at work on Miss Oliver's portrait. The head was finished already, and there was only the background to color.

While I was busy with this task, there was a tap at the door, and St. John Rivers entered. "I have come to see how you are spending your holiday," he said. "Ah, I see you've been drawing. Good! That should keep you from getting lonely."

St. John stooped to examine my drawing. However, when he saw that it was a picture of Miss Oliver, he sprang back as if he had been staring into the eyes of the lady herself.

Said I to myself, "I am sure it would do him good to talk a little about this sweet Rosamond, from whom he runs like a hare fleeing from a hunter. I will make him talk."

Said I to him, "Take a chair, Mr. Rivers." But he answered, as he always did, that he could not stay.

Said I to myself, "Very well. Stand if you like, but I'm not going to let you leave just yet. I must try to find out your secret feeling toward Miss Oliver."

"Is this picture like her?" I asked him suddenly.

"Like her? Like whom? I did not look at it closely," he replied.

"Yes, you did, Mr. Rivers. You looked at it closely and carefully, but I have no objection to your looking at it again." As I said that, I rose and placed the portrait in his hand.

"The picture is well done," he said. "The coloring is very soft and clear. The drawing is very graceful and correct."

"Yes, yes, I know all that. But whom is it like?"

After some hesitation he answered, "Miss Oliver, I suppose."

"Of course. And now, sir, to reward you for the accurate guess, I will promise to paint for you a good duplicate of this picture. That is, I'll do so if you wish it. I don't want to throw away my time and trouble on something you would think worthless."

He continued to gaze at the picture. The longer he looked, the more he seemed to like it. "It is very much like her!" he murmured. "The features are perfect. The face smiles!"

"Would it please you to have a painting like it? When you are in India, will it bring you pleasant or unpleasant memories?"

"Pleasant and unpleasant, both. But certainly I should like to have it."

"If that is so," I declared, "then why be content with only a picture? Why not take Miss Oliver to India as your wife? She likes you, I am sure."

"*Does* she like me?" he asked.

"Oh, yes. Better than she likes anyone else. She talks of you continually. There is no subject she enjoys so much or mentions so often."

"Perhaps you would think it strange," he said, "that while I love Rosamond Oliver, I still believe that she would not make a good wife for me. She is not suited to me."

"That is strange, indeed!" I exclaimed.

"A missionary lives a hard life. He does not enjoy the comforts and conveniences of life in England. His wife must be willing to undergo a great many hardships, and Rosamond could never do that. Rosamond could never be a missionary's wife."

"But you need not be a missionary. You can give up that scheme."

"What! Give up the great work I want to do? It is dearer than the blood in my veins. Sometimes a man's work is more important to him than anything else. It is so with me. My work is what I look forward to and live for."

Now I understood why he had acted so queerly toward Rosamond. "But aren't Miss Oliver's feelings important?" I asked. "Aren't her disappointment and sorrow of any importance to you?"

"Miss Oliver is always surrounded by young men," he said coolly. "In a month after I have gone, I shall be out of her heart. She will forget me and probably marry someone who will make her far happier than I could."

Having said this, he took his hat, which lay on the table beside my brushes. Once more he looked at the portrait.

"She *is* beautiful," he murmured. "Her name fits her very well. *Rosamond* means Rose of the World. It describes her perfectly, indeed."

"And may I not paint a picture like this for you?"

"What's the good? No."

St. John seemed scarcely able to tear his glance from the painting, but now at last he began to turn away. At this point, however, something happened which left me wondering for days afterward. Near the picture was a sheet of thin paper on which I used to rest my hand while painting, in order to protect the cardboard underneath from getting dirty. The paper was entirely blank, or so I thought. What he suddenly saw on it, I could not tell. Still, something had caught his eye. He took it up with a quick snatch. First he looked at the edge, and then he shot a glance at me. His expression was very peculiar and difficult to understand. His eyes took in all the details of my appearance from head to foot. His lips parted as if he were about to speak, but then he checked himself and held back the remark, whatever it was.

"What is the matter?" I asked.

"Nothing at all," he replied. Yet as he put down the paper, I saw him secretly tearing a narrow piece from the margin. As it disappeared into his glove, he nodded hastily and started for the door. His hurry was so great that he did not even stop as he called back over his shoulder, "Good afternoon, Miss Elliot."

When he had gone, I looked carefully at the paper. On it I saw nothing but a few stains where I had tried out a color. "Well!" I exclaimed. "This is a new mystery."

17

One evening some time after St. John's mysterious action I was sitting at my fireside, reading a book. Outside there was a swirling snowstorm, but I was comfortable enough beside my warm fire, dreamily enjoying the magic world of the story on the printed page.

My shutter was closed, and I had laid a mat at the door to prevent the snow from blowing under it. Still I thought I heard a noise from outside. Could it be the wind shaking the door? No, it was St. John Rivers, who, lifting the latch, came in out of the freezing snow. As he entered from the howling blackness of the night, he looked almost like a ghost. The cloak that covered his tall figure was all white with snow. So little had I expected any guest from the blocked-up valley that I was quite frightened until I recognized my visitor.

"Any bad news?" I demanded. "Has anything happened?"

"No. How very easily you become upset!" he answered, removing his cloak and hanging it up against the door. After this he calmly stamped the snow from his boots and pushed the mat back in place to keep out the draft.

"I am getting your floor full of snow and mud," said he, "but you must forgive me for once." Then he approached the fire. "I have had hard work to get here, I assure you," he remarked as he warmed his hands over the flame. "I fell in one drift up to the waist, but fortunately the snow is quite soft yet."

He seemed in no hurry to explain the reason for his calling to see me on such a night, and I was so anxious to hear it that I neglected ordinary politeness. "But why have you come?" I could not help saying.

"That's rather an inhospitable question to ask a visitor. Since you ask it, however, my answer is that I simply must have a little talk with you. For one thing, I have grown tired of my silent books and empty rooms. Besides, since yesterday I have been filled with excitement by a story I heard."

"It must be a very thrilling tale," I told him, "for you are scarcely one to be easily excited. Have you really come out in this dreadful storm just to tell it to me?"

He smiled and looked at me rather queerly. "The

truth is," said he, "I have heard only half the tale, and I am impatient to hear the rest. That's why I have come to you."

Upon saying this, he sat down as if intending to stay for the evening. I thought back to his peculiar actions on the day I had showed him Miss Oliver's picture, and I began to fear that he was out of his wits. I waited, expecting that he would say something I could understand, but he leaned on his elbow and appeared to be lost in thought.

Finally I spoke. "Surely you did not expect to get the ending from me."

"That is exactly what I do expect," St. John said quietly. "Let me begin. Then perhaps you will finish the story for me. I should warn you, however, that much of it will sound old to you."

"Please don't tease me!" I cried. "You have awakened my interest. Tell me the tale."

"Well, twenty years ago," he began, "a poor young man fell in love with a rich man's daughter. I shall not mention their names just yet, for that would be getting ahead of my story. But, to continue, the rich young lady returned his love, and they were married. Her father and friends, however, did not favor the marriage, and so would have nothing to do with them after the wedding. Luck, too, was against them. In another two years both fell sick of a terrible illness and died almost at the same time. They left a baby daughter, who was cared for by charity organizations. Does my story, thus far, sound at all familiar to you, Miss Elliot?"

"I am not sure yet whether I have ever heard it before," I replied, but my voice was not steady, for the tale he told *did* begin to sound familiar.

"Let me proceed, then," he went on. "At the age of

ten the orphan was sent to Lowood School. There she became a fine pupil, and later a teacher. But life at the school was too dull, and she decided to find herself a position elsewhere. By advertising, she found work as a governess. Consequently, she left Lowood and went to teach a little girl in the home of a certain Mr. Rochester."

"Oh, Mr. Rivers!" I exclaimed, with my breath catching in my throat.

"I can guess how you feel," he said, "but be quiet for just a moment more. I have nearly finished. Hear my story to the end. About Mr. Rochester I know very little, but I imagine that he was a low villain. It is said that he tried to marry this young girl although he had a wife still alive. Only when they already stood at the altar in the church was his secret revealed. Just what happened to the girl afterwards is not known. During the night she left Thornfield Hall and disappeared. Thornfield Hall, by the way, was the name of Mr. Rochester's home. I think I forgot to tell you that. Mr. Rochester and others searched the country for her far and wide, but could get not a single scrap of information regarding her whereabouts. Yet something has happened that makes it extremely important for her to be found."

"Has this happening anything to do with Mr. Rochester?" I inquired.

"No, it has more to do with a lawyer named Briggs. He has put advertisements in all the papers. In fact, I myself have just received a letter from him, giving all the details I have told you. Isn't it an odd tale?"

"Just tell me this," said I, "and since you know so much, you surely can tell it to me—what about Mr. Rochester? How and where is he? What is he doing? Is he well?" Somehow at that moment I was not half so anxious to know what Mr. Briggs wanted with me, as to be told how my dear Mr. Rochester was and what had happened to him since I had left Thornfield Hall.

"I know nothing about Mr. Rochester. The letter does not mention him except to tell of his unlawful attempt at marriage, of which I have already spoken. Why don't you ask, instead, for the name of the governess? Why don't you ask the reason for Mr. Briggs's interest in her?" Mr. Rivers looked closely at me, but I did not choose to answer his inquiries.

"In seeking information about this girl," I questioned, "didn't Mr. Briggs go to Thornfield Hall? Didn't he see Mr. Rochester?"

"I suppose not."

"But Mr. Briggs wrote to him, surely."

"Of course."

"And what was the reply? Who has the letters?"

"Mr. Briggs says that the answer was not from Mr. Rochester, but from a lady who was evidently a servant."

I felt cold and dismayed. My worst fears then were probably true. Mr. Rochester had, no doubt, left England and gone back to his old wicked life. Oh, my poor master—who had once almost been my husband—my poor Edward! This I cried in my heart, but said none of it aloud.

"He must have been a bad man," remarked Mr. Rivers.

"Don't give an opinion about him," I said angrily. "You don't know him."

"Very well," he answered quietly. "In any case, my head is occupied with other matters. I have my tale to finish. Since you won't ask the name of the governess, I must tell it of my own accord. Let me see—I have it here. It is always more satisfactory to see important points written down in black and white."

Mr. Rivers drew forth his wallet and took from it a shabby slip of paper. I recognized it as the one which he had torn off while visiting me, and which he had so mysteriously carried away. He got up and held it close to my eyes. I read, in my own handwriting, the words "Jane Eyre." Probably while thinking of something else, I had absentmindedly scribbled down my *real* name on that sheet of paper.

"You must remember," he said, "the day I called on you, when you showed me Miss Oliver's picture. On glancing at a paper on your table, I noticed this signature and realized that you had accidently given yourself away. Your true name was Jane Eyre, not Jane Elliot. Once I knew that, I began to make inquiries about you. I wrote to the school which you had mentioned as the one in which you had taught. They answered, giving a high opinion of you. In their reply they stated that they had recently been questioned regarding your whereabouts by a Mr. Briggs. Immediately I sent a letter to him, and as I have said, his answer gave me the details of the story I've just told you."

"Yes, yes," I cried, "but where is Mr. Briggs? Perhaps he knows more about Mr. Rochester than you do."

"Briggs is in London. I doubt whether he knows anything at all about Mr. Rochester, for it is not Mr. Rochester in whom he is interested. Meanwhile, you are forgetting essential points while paying attention to trifles. You do not inquire why Mr. Briggs searched for you—what he wanted with you."

"Well, what did he want?"

"Merely to tell you that your uncle, Mr. Eyre of Madeira, is dead. Mr. Briggs is merely anxious to tell you that your uncle has left you all his property, and that you are now rich—merely that—and nothing more."

"Left it to me? I am rich?"

"Yes, you are an heiress—and quite rich."

Silence followed, while I tried to get accustomed to this new idea.

"You must prove your identity, of course," continued St. John presently, "but that is a step which will offer no difficulties. You can then enter on immediate possession of your fortune. Briggs has the will and the necessary documents."

Here was a new card turned up in the game of Fate! It was a fine thing to be lifted in a moment from poverty to wealth—a very fine thing, but it was not a pleasure that I could begin to enjoy at a moment's notice. I did not jump and spring and shout "Hurrah" at hearing that I had been left a fortune. For one matter, my uncle, my only relative, was dead. I had always hoped to see him some day. Now I never should. For another matter, the money came only to me. I had no family to rejoice with me. Still it was a great blessing, and the independence it gave me would be glorious.

"You are beginning to smile at last," said Mr. Rivers. "I almost thought you were unhappy at hearing this news. Perhaps now you will ask how much you are worth."

"How much am I worth?"

"Oh, a trifle! Nothing to speak of—twenty thousand pounds I think it is—but what is that?"

"Twenty thousand pounds?"

Here was a new surprise. I had been calculating on four or five thousand. This information actually took away my breath for a moment. Mr. St. John, whom I had never heard laugh aloud before, laughed now.

"Well," said he, "if you had committed a murder, and I had told you your crime was discovered, you could scarcely look more horrified."

"It is a large sum. Don't you think there is a mistake?"

"No mistake at all."

"Perhaps you have read the figures wrong. It may be 2,000—not 20,000."

"It is written in letters, not figures—twenty thousand."

The thought of having so much wealth made me very uncomfortable. I felt like a person of but average appetite, sitting down to feast alone at a table spread with food for a hundred.

"Since you will have much business to take care of," said St. John, "I have already made arrangements for someone else to take charge of the school for the time being. In any event, I doubt that you will care to continue in your present position, now that you are a rich woman." He looked at me questioningly.

"I don't know," I declared. "Perhaps I shall stay and continue teaching my girls. What better way can I spend my time? What else shall I find to occupy myself in Morton? And where else can I go? Here I have a few friends and my pupils, who like me and keep me from being altogether lonely."

"If you knew what it is to possess and enjoy wealth," replied St. John, "you would speak otherwise. You have no idea of the importance twenty thousand pounds will give you. You don't know the place it will enable you to take in society. You can't imagine the opportunities it will provide for you."

"No, Mr. Rivers, you are wrong. I have lived with

wealthy people. I know it is pleasant to have money, but other things may be even more valuable."

After I spoke these words, St. John cast a piercing glance at me, as if trying to gaze into my heart. Getting up, he walked back and forth across the room. He was evidently deep in thought. At last he stopped and turned toward me again.

"Jane," he said, "you speak of your friends in Morton as if they mattered a great deal to you. Have you ever thought that you might find among them the dearest friend of all, a husband?"

I blushed deeply, for while his question had taken me by surprise, I could foretell what his next words were likely to be.

"Jane, I am leaving England in six weeks. I have already engaged passage on a ship. Let me make arrangements for another passenger. Come with me to India. Come as my wife and fellow missionary."

"Oh, St. John," I cried, "I have not even dreamed of such a possibility. How can I answer you? I always thought you would marry Rosamond, if you married anyone."

"No," he said firmly, "she is not for me. It is you whom I have chosen, because you have the qualities to work for the good of your fellow human beings. Nature intended you for a missionary's wife. The fact that as a wealthy woman you are willing to remain in Morton and teach the villagers' children shows your character. Come with me, and we shall work together. For myself, I do not care a whit about your money, but in India it can do great good. Of course, you know that I am not a fortune-hunter, Jane. With or without your riches, I should still want you to be my wife and fellow worker."

St. John came and stood behind my chair. He placed his hand upon my shoulder as if already he claimed me as his own. My thoughts were in a whirl. "Surely," I said to myself, "St. John wants me as a fellow worker more than as a wife. He does not have the feeling for me that a husband should have for a wife. Nor do I feel toward him as a wife should, to her husband. Nevertheless, it may be all for the best. Perhaps this is the proper path for me to take. Oh, if only Heaven were to give me a sign to show what is right for me to do!"

I was more excited than I had ever been before. Therefore, it may be that what took place next was simply the result of too much excitement and imagination. But, whatever the cause, it was the most amazing happening of my whole life.

All the house was still. The room was half in darkness, for the fire had died down. My heart beat so fast and loud that I seemed to hear its throb. Suddenly it stood still, as a strange feeling thrilled my body. The sensation was not like an electric shock, but it was quite as sharp, as strange, as startling. It acted on my senses as if they had been asleep and were now, in a flash, forced to wake. My nerves jumped to alertness. As if expecting a message, my eyes and ears waited, while the flesh quivered on my bones.

"What have you heard? What do you see?" asked St. John.

I saw nothing, but I heard a voice somewhere cry, "Jane! Jane! Jane!" then there was nothing more.

"Oh, Heaven! What is it?" I gasped.

I might have said, "Where is it?" It did not seem in the room—nor in the house—nor in the garden. It did not come out of the air—nor from under the earth —nor from overhead. I had heard it, but from where or how it came was impossible to know! And it was the voice of a human being, a known, loved, and well-remembered voice: that of Edward Fairfax Rochester. It spoke wildly, strangely, and urgently, as if in pain and sorrow.

"I am coming!" I cried. "Wait for me! Oh, I will come!" I flew to the door, and looked into the passage, but it was dark. I ran out into the garden, but it was empty.

"Where are you?" I exclaimed.

The hills beyond Marsh Glen echoed the answer faintly, "Where are you?" I listened. The wind sighed low in the firs. All was loneliness and midnight hush. The storm had ceased.

"This cannot be the influence of superstition!" I commented as I stood beside the gate. "This is no witch-craft. It is the work of nature. She was called upon and did not a miracle, but her best."

I broke from St. John, who had followed and would have detained me. It was *my* time to take command. I told him to offer no questions or remarks, and asked him to leave me, for I desired to be alone. He obeyed at once. Where there is power to command well enough, obedience never fails. I went up to my room and locked myself in. There, after making up my mind, I lay down to await the daylight with the greatest eagerness.

18

The daylight came. I rose at dawn. "Before many days have passed," I said to myself, "I must learn what has happened to Mr. Rochester. There is no doubt in my mind that his voice called me last night."

By afternoon I was ready to set out on my journey, which would take thirty-six hours. It was Tuesday when I started, and early on the following Thursday morning, the coachman stopped to water his horses at a familiar wayside inn.

"How far is Thornfield Hall from here?" I asked of the stable man.

"Just two miles, ma'am, across the fields."

"My journey is nearly finished," I thought to myself. I got out of the coach and gave my bag to the innkeeper to hold till I called for it. As I left the inn, the light of dawn gleamed on its sign, and I read in gilt letters, "The Rochester Arms." My heart leaped up as I realized that I was already on my master's lands. Then it fell again as the thought came: "Your master himself may be across the English Channel, for all you know. Besides, if he is at Thornfield Hall, who is there with him? His lunatic wife! You are wasting your time, and you had better go no farther."

Still I could not stop. Out I hurried into the fields, by the shortest way to Thornfield Hall. How fast I walked! How anxiously I looked for my first glimpse of my former home! I longed to see its solid walls and handsome towers. "I shall view it first from the front," I thought. "There I shall be able to see my master's own window. Since he is an early riser, he may already be standing at it. Or he may now be walking in the orchard or on the pavement in front. If I could but see him for a moment! Let me just find out whether all is well with him, and I can go away content. Then I shall know that I only imagined the voice I heard calling me in the night."

I had passed along the lower wall of the orchard, and now turned a corner. Just there was a gate between two thick stone posts. From behind one of these heavy pillars I could peep round quietly at the full front of the mansion. Wishing to remain unseen, I advanced my head carefully into a position where I could observe whether the curtains were pulled back from any of the bedroom windows.

The morning was clear, and there was no mist to bar my view. Joyfully I gazed, expecting to see the splendid beauties of the old house that I remembered so well. But what I saw was a blackened ruin!

No need for me to hide behind a gatepost! No need to peep up at windows, fearing to find an old friend looking out! No need to listen for doors opening or for steps on the pavement! Thornfield Hall was empty! It had no people, no rooms, no furnishings, no chimneys, no roof! The front was like the wall of a shell, with paneless windows that opened into nothing, for all had crashed in!

And there was the silence of death about it. The mournful blackness of the stones told me what had destroyed the Hall—fire. All that was not made of stone had burned to the ground. But how had the flames been kindled? What was the story of this disaster? What had been lost besides plaster, marble, and woodwork? Had life been wrecked, as well as property? If so, whose? There was no one here to reply to my dreadful questions.

I decided to try to find the answer at the inn, and there I returned. The host himself brought my breakfast into the parlor. I requested him to shut the door and sit down, since I had some questions to ask him.

"You know Thornfield Hall, of course?" I inquired.

"Yes, ma'am," he replied. "I lived there once."

"Did you?" I said, thinking to myself that he could not have lived there while I was at the Hall, for he was a stranger to me.

"I was the late Mr. Rochester's butler," he added.

"The late Mr. Rochester!" I gasped. "Is he dead?"

"I mean that I was butler to the father of the present Mr. Rochester. Mr. Edward Rochester's father has been dead for many years, but Mr. Edward himself is still a young man and should have many years of life before him."

My heart had stood still when I thought my dear master dead, but now my blood continued its flow once more and I breathed freely again. *My* Mr. Rochester at least was alive.

"Is Mr. Rochester living at Thornfield Hall now?" I asked. Although I knew that my master was no longer at the Hall, I hoped to get further information by this question.

"No, ma'am—oh, no! No one is living there. I suppose you are a stranger in these parts, or you would have heard what happened last autumn. Thornfield Hall is quite a ruin. It was burnt down just about harvest time. A dreadful calamity! Such an immense quantity of valuable property destroyed! Hardly any of the furniture could be saved. The fire broke out at dead of night, and before the engines arrived from Millcote, the building was one mass of flame. It was a terrible spectacle. I witnessed it myself."

"At dead of night!" I muttered. Yes, that was always the hour of trouble at Thornfield. "Was it known how it started?" I demanded.

"They guessed, ma'am. They guessed. Indeed, I should say it was learned beyond a doubt. You are not perhaps aware," he continued, edging his chair a little nearer the table and speaking low, "that there was a lady—a lunatic—kept in the house?"

"I have heard something of it."

"She was kept under lock and key, ma'am. People even for years were not absolutely certain of her existence. No one saw her. They only knew by rumor that such a person was at the Hall. Who or what she was it was difficult to guess. They said Mr. Edward had brought her from some other country. But a queer thing happened a year ago—a very queer thing."

I feared now that he would tell my own story. I tried to keep him to the main subject.

"And this lady?" I asked.

"This lady, ma'am," he answered, "turned out to be Mr. Rochester's wife! The discovery was brought about in the strangest way. There was a young lady, a governess at the Hall, that Mr. Rochester fell in—"

"But tell me about the fire," I interrupted, much embarrassed at this turn of the talk.

"I'm coming to that, ma'am. There was a young lady that Mr. Edward fell in love with. The servants say they never saw anybody so much in love as he was. He was after her continually. They used to watch him —servants will, you know—and he set his heart on her above everything. She was a little small thing, they say, almost like a child. I never saw her myself, but I've heard Leah, the housemaid, tell of her. Leah liked her well enough. Now, you see, this young lady was at the altar with Mr. Rochester, being married, when—"

"You shall tell me this part of the story another time," I said, "but now I have a particular reason for wanting to hear all about the fire. Was it suspected that this lunatic, Mrs. Rochester, had any hand in it?"

"You've hit it, ma'am. It's quite certain that it was her, and nobody but her, that set it going. She had a woman to take care of her, called Mrs. Poole. This nurse was an able woman in her line, and very trustworthy but for one fault. She kept a private bottle of gin by her, and now and then took a drop too much. It is not excusable, except that she had a hard life of it. Besides, it was dangerous, for Mrs. Poole would fall fast asleep, and the mad lady, who was as cunning as a witch, would take the keys out of her pocket. Then she would let herself out of her room and go roaming about the house, doing any wild mischief that came into her head. They say she had nearly burnt her husband in his bed once, but I don't know about that. However, on this night, she set fire first to the hangings of the room next to hers. Then she got down to a lower story and made her way to the chamber that had been the governess's, and she kindled the bed there. Fortunately there was nobody sleeping in it. The governess had run away two months before."

"Was Mr. Rochester at home," I broke in, "when the fire started?"

"Yes, indeed he was. He went up to the attic when all was burning above and below, and got the servants out of their beds and helped them down himself. Then he went back to get his mad wife out of her cell. And then they called out to him that she was on the roof.

There she was standing, waving her arms and shouting out till they could hear her a mile off. I saw and heard her with my own eyes. She was a big woman and had long, black hair. We could see it streaming against the flames as she stood. I witnessed, and several more witnessed Mr. Rochester climb through the skylight onto the roof. We heard him call, 'Bertha!' We saw him approach her. And then she yelled and gave a spring, and the next minute she lay smashed on the pavement."

"Dead?"

"Dead? Ay, dead as the stones on which her brains and blood were scattered."

"Good heavens!"

"You may well say so, ma'am. It was frightful!" He shuddered.

"And afterwards?" I urged.

"Well, ma'am, afterwards the house was burnt to the ground. There are only some bits of walls standing now."

"Were there any other lives lost?" I asked.

"No—perhaps it would have been better if there had."

"What do you mean?"

"Poor Mr. Edward!" he exclaimed. "I little thought ever to have seen it! Some say it was a just judgment on him for keeping his first marriage secret, and wanting to take another wife while he had one living. But, for my part, I pity him."

"You said he was alive?" I asked anxiously.

"Yes, yes. He is alive, but many think he would be better dead."

"Why? How?" My blood was again running cold. "Where is he?" I demanded. "Is he in England?"

"Ay—ay—he's in England. He can't get out of England, I fancy. He's a fixture, now."

What agony it was to hear this! And the man seemed in no hurry to explain further.

"He is stone blind," the innkeeper said at last. "Yes —he is stone blind—is Mr. Edward."

I had dreaded worse. I had dreaded that he was mad. I finally found the strength to ask what had caused this calamity.

"It was all his own courage and his kindness, in a way, ma'am. He wouldn't leave the house till everyone else was out before him. As he came down the great staircase at last, after Mrs. Rochester had flung herself from the roof, there was a great crash—all fell. He was taken out from under the ruins, alive but sadly hurt. A beam had fallen in such a way as to protect him partly. But one eye was knocked out, and one hand so crushed that Mr. Carter, the doctor, had to amputate it at once. The other eye became inflamed, and he lost the sight of that also. He is now helpless indeed—blind and a cripple."

"Where is he? Where does he now live?"

"At Ferndean, a farm he has. It's about thirty miles off and quite a lonely spot."

"Who is with him?"

"Old John and his wife. He would have no one else. He is quite broken down, they say."

"Have you any sort of carriage?"

"We have a chaise, ma'am, a very handsome chaise."

"Let it be made ready immediately. If your carriage boy can drive me to Ferndean before dark this day, I'll pay both you and him twice the hire you usually demand."

19

Thus at last I came to my master's house. When I knocked at the door, John's wife opened it for me.

"Mary," I said, "how are you?"

She started back as if she had seen a ghost, but I calmed her. "Is it really you, miss," she said, "come at this late hour to this lonely place?" I answered by taking her hand. Then I followed her into the kitchen, where John was sitting by a good fire. I explained to them, in a few words, that I had heard all which had happened since I left Thornfield, and that I had come to see Mr. Rochester. Just at this moment the parlor bell rang.

"When you go in," said I, "tell your master that a person wishes to speak to him. But do not give my name."

"I don't think he will see you," she answered. "He refuses everybody."

When she returned, I inquired what he had said.

"You are to send in your name and your business," she replied. She then proceeded to fill a glass with water, and place it on a tray together with candles.

"Is that what he rang for?" I asked.

"Yes. He always has candles brought in as it gets dark, even though he is blind."

"Give me the tray," I requested. "I will carry it in."

I took it from her hand, and she pointed out the parlor door to me. As I held it, the tray shook and the water spilled from the glass. My heart struck my ribs loud and fast. Mary opened the door for me and shut it again after I had passed through.

The parlor looked gloomy. Leaning over close to a small fire was my blind master. His old dog, Pilot, lay on one side out of the way, coiled up as if afraid of being accidentally stepped on. Pilot pricked up his ears when I came in. Then he jumped up with a yelp and a whine, and bounded towards me. He almost knocked the tray from my hands. I set it on the table, then patted him and said softly, "Lie down!" Mr. Rochester turned automatically as if to *see* what the trouble was, but as he could see nothing, he simply sighed and returned to his first position.

His injured arm he kept half hidden in the front of his coat. The other he held out toward me. "Give me the water, Mary," he said.

I approached him with the glass. Pilot followed me, still excited.

"What is the matter?" he inquired.

"Down, Pilot!" I said again. He checked the water on its way to his lips, and seemed to listen. He drank and put the glass down. "That is you, Mary, is it not?"

"Mary is in the kitchen," I answered.

He put out his hand with a quick gesture, but not seeing where I stood, he did not touch me. "Who is it? Who is it?" he demanded, trying—as it seemed—to see with those sightless eyes. "Answer me—speak again!" he ordered.

"Will you have a little more water, sir? I spilled half of what was in the glass," I said.

"Who is it? Who speaks?"

"Pilot knows me, and John and Mary know I am here. I came only this evening," I answered.

"Great Scott! What sweet madness has come over me?" he cried. He stretched out his hand, and I caught it in mine.

"Her own fingers!" he exclaimed. "Her small, slender fingers! If they are here, there must be more of her."

His muscular hand broke from my grasp. My arm was seized, and then my shoulder—neck—waist. His arms came round and gathered me to him. "It *is* Jane? She *is* here?"

"She is all here," I said joyfully. "God bless you, sir! I am glad to be so near you again."

"Jane Eyre! Jane Eyre," was all he said.

"My dear master," I answered, "I am Jane Eyre. I have found you—I have come back to you."

"In truth? In the flesh? My living Jane?"

"You hold me tightly enough, sir. I am not like empty air, am I?"

"My living darling! These are certainly her arms, and these are her features. But I cannot be so blessed after all my misery. It is a dream such as I often have had. I have dreamed that I once more held her to my heart, as I do now—and kissed her, as I do now. It is you—is it, Jane? You have come back to me, then?"

"I have."

"Ah, Jane, how have you been? I had a search made for you everywhere. I pictured you poor and alone, depending on the kindness of strangers."

"Oh, sir, I have become an independent woman now."

"Independent! What do you mean, Jane?"

"My uncle in Madeira is dead, and he left me twenty thousand pounds."

"What, Jane? Are you a rich woman?"

"Quite rich, sir. If you won't let me live with you, I can build a house of my own close up to your door, and you may come and sit in my parlor when you want company of an evening."

"Jane, Jane, how I felt when I discovered you had gone from Thornfield. On examining your room, I found that you had taken very little. The pearl necklace I gave you had been left behind in its little box. Your trunks were locked and untouched, just as they had been prepared for our wedding trip. You must have had almost no money. What could my darling do, I wondered, left alone and penniless? And what did you do? Let me hear now."

Thus invited, I began the story of my experiences. I proceeded to tell him of how I got my position as schoolteacher, of my life in the village, and of how I received the news of my inheritance. Of course, the name of St. John Rivers was mentioned often during the course of my tale. When I had finished my story, Mr. Rochester at once began to question me about St. John.

"You have spoken of this man Rivers often. Do you like him?"

"He is a very good man, sir. I could not help but like him."

"No doubt he is an old man," said Mr. Rochester. "About fifty years of age, I suppose."

"St. John is only twenty-nine, sir," I replied, smiling to myself. I could see that my master was beginning to be jealous.

"Ah," said he, "I forget what description you gave of his appearance—probably a homely looking fellow, full of stiff manners and half-choked by his collar."

"St. John dresses well. He is a handsome man—tall, fair, with blue eyes and a generally excellent appearance."

"Confound him!" said Mr. Rochester to himself. Then he asked a question of me, "Perhaps you would rather not sit on my knee any longer, Miss Eyre?"

That was the pleasant position where I was seated, but I had no intention of leaving it. "Why should I not sit there, Mr. Rochester?" I asked.

"Jane," replied my master, "when you can go to such a man as St. John Rivers, why should you stay with me? Why do you remain here, sitting on my knee, Jane?"

"Because I am comfortable there."

"No, Jane, you cannot be comfortable there. Your heart is not with me. It is with this St. John. Oh, till this moment I thought my little Jane was all mine! But it is useless to grieve. Jane, leave me. Go and marry Rivers."

"I will not go, sir. He does not love me. I do not love him. He is good and great, but cold as an iceberg. He is not like you, sir. I am not happy at his side."

"What, Jane! Is this true?"

"Absolutely, sir. Oh, you need not be jealous! All my heart is yours, sir."

He kissed me again, but his face was sad. "If only I were not blind and crippled!" he cried. "I am no better than the old chestnut tree which was struck by lightning in Thornfield orchard. What right have I to take a wife?"

"Every right, sir," I replied, "as long as she is willing to marry you."

"Jane, will you marry me?"

"Yes, sir."

"A poor blind man, whom you will have to wait on?"

"Yes, sir."

"On this arm I have no hand," he said, taking the crushed limb out of his coat. "It is a horrible sight! Don't you think so, Jane?"

"It is a pity to see it—and a pity to see your eyes—and the scar of the fire on your forehead. But I want to be your wife nonetheless."

"Oh, my darling Jane! God bless and reward you!"

"Mr. Rochester, if ever I did a good deed in my life, I am rewarded now. Because I am to be your wife, I am as happy as I can be on earth."

"Jane, there is something I must tell you. It is a strange thing. Last Monday night I was sitting in my room and thinking of you. I thought of how I had once said to you that I would give up the sinful life I lived. And I thought to myself that I had indeed kept my word. Your influence had led me to a good way of life. From the day we had spoken of it together, I had turned away from my old wicked habits."

Mr. Rochester stopped speaking for a moment, and I said, "But what is strange about that?"

"I am only coming to the strange part," he answered. "It suddenly came to me that perhaps I had not been leading such a good life, after all. Of course, since our talk I had done nothing wicked or sinful. But what had I done that was good? What had I done for others? Had I helped the tenants on my land? Had I assisted the poor people in the nearby villages? Had I done anything for the people of my country? Had I done anything for my fellow man? It seemed to me that if only I were not blind and crippled, I would use all my powers for the good of others. And then I thought that if I had you by my side, Jane, I could do these things. My heart grew full of longing for you, and I cried out, 'Jane! Jane! Jane!' "

"Did you speak those words aloud?" I asked.

"I did, Jane."

"And it was last Monday night, some time near midnight?"

"Yes, but that doesn't matter. The strange thing is what happened afterward. Perhaps you will think me superstitious. Still I tell you that this is true. After I cried out 'Jane! Jane! Jane!'—a voice replied, 'I am coming. Wait for me. Where are you?' And the voice was yours, Jane."

"Oh, my love," I said, "I heard your call and you heard mine. I do not know what made it possible, but surely our marriage is favored on earth and in heaven."

20

I have now been married ten years. I know what it is to live with one I love best on earth. I consider myself blessed because I am part of my husband's life as fully as he is part of mine.

Little Adele has grown up. During her childhood I sent her to an excellent school, which gave her a sound education. I took care that she never lacked anything for her comfort, and she was always happy and made fair progress in her studies. When she left school and came home, I found her a pleasing and obliging companion. She is good-tempered, well-mannered, and of fine character. By her grateful attention to me, she has long ago repaid any little kindness I ever did her.

As to St. John Rivers, he left England and went to India. There he is faithfully carrying on his good work. St. John is unmarried. He says that he will never marry now.

My husband, too, has been doing great and good things. He has helped to pass laws for the benefit of the working people and farmers of England. He has fought for the rights of all men. With me at his side, he has done what he had hoped to do for his fellow man.

Mr. Rochester continued to be blind for the first two years of our marriage. He saw everything through my eyes, for I described each scene that lay before us. Never did I weary of taking him where he wished to go or of doing for him what he wished to be done. There was a pleasure in my duty, even though it was sad.

One morning, at the end of two years, he came and bent over me and said, "Jane, have you a glittering ornament around your neck?"

I had on a gold watch chain. I answered, "Yes."

"And have you a pale blue dress on?"

I had. He informed me then that sight was returning to one eye.

He and I went up to London. My husband got the advice of a great doctor, and he eventually recovered the sight of that one eye. He cannot see now very distinctly. He cannot read or write much, but he can see without being led by the hand. When his first-born child was put into his arms, he could see that the boy had inherited his own eyes as they once were—large, brilliant, and black.

My Edward and I, then, are happy. We have our son and each other, and that is everything we want.

The End

REVIEWING YOUR READING

CHAPTER 1

FINDING THE MAIN IDEA

1. Which title tells most about the chapter?
(A) "The Long Ride to Thornfield Hall" (B) "A Warm Welcome, A Cold Corridor" (C) "A Pleasant Old Lady"
(D) "A New Job, An Old House"

REMEMBERING DETAIL

2. During her ride to Thornfield Hall, Jane Eyre
(A) imagines what Mrs. Fairfax will be like (B) complains to the driver that he is going too slow (C) sings songs to help pass the time (D) writes a letter to Mrs. Fairfax
3. How many other people at Thornfield Hall does Mrs. Fairfax mention?
(A) Two (B) Three (C) Five (D) Ten
4. The corridor leading to the bedrooms is all of these EXCEPT
(A) drafty (B) gloomy (C) church-like (D) well-lighted

DRAWING CONCLUSIONS

5. You can tell that before Jane came to Thornfield Hall, she
(A) worked as a housemaid (B) never had been a governess (C) had several offers of marriage (D) always lived by herself

USING YOUR REASON

6. The job of a governess is most like that of a
(A) nurse (B) politician (C) housekeeper (D) teacher
7. Which of the following is the most illogical part of the chapter?
(A) That the driver would let his horse walk so slowly
(B) That Mrs. Fairfax would offer Jane a hot drink and sandwiches (C) That Jane would feel frightened after such a pleasant welcome (D) That Jane would have a room all to herself

IDENTIFYING THE MOOD

8. Which of the following best describes Jane's responses to Mrs. Fairfax?
   (A) Arrogant   (B) Joyful   (C) Polite   (D) Worshipful

READING FOR DEEPER MEANING

9. The chapter suggests that which of the following is important in the world of *Jane Eyre?*
   (A) Knowing your place   (B) Getting rich quickly
   (C) Dying for your country   (D) Fighting for equality

THINKING IT OVER

1. Jane is a bit puzzled by Mrs. Fairfax's warm welcome. Jane says, "I felt rather confused at receiving so much attention from my employer." What does this tell you about employer/employee relationships during the period this book takes place? Further, what might this tell you about Mrs. Fairfax?
2. Jane doesn't tell us much about herself. What does she tell us? What can you guess about her? For example, how old do you think she is? What makes you think so? Where do you think Jane comes from? How would you describe her personality? Is she strong or weak? How can you tell?

CHAPTER 2

FINDING THE MAIN IDEA

1. This chapter is mostly about how Jane
   (A) begins to dislike Mrs. Fairfax   (B)speaks in French with her pupil, Adele   (C) gazes out at the countryside around Thornfield Hall   (D) learns new things about Thornfield Hall

REMEMBERING DETAIL

2. Who is the owner of Thornfield Hall?
   (A) Grace Poole   (B) Mrs. Fairfax   (C) George Bernard Thornfield   (D) Edward Fairfax Rochester
3. Mrs. Fairfax says that Mr. Rochester is
   (A) peculiar, but a very good master   (B) cruel and a heavy drinker   (C) blond and blue-eyed   (D) happy, but rather stupid

4. While walking in the third-floor corridor, Jane
(A) meets Adele for the second time (B) trips on the
carpet and almost falls (C) hears a strange laugh
(D) sees what she thinks is a ghost

DRAWING CONCLUSIONS
5. You can tell from the chapter that Jane
(A) has met Mr. Rochester before (B) has some talent
in art (C) is not really interested in teaching (D) speaks
Spanish as well as English

USING YOUR REASON
6. When Adele says that her mother "is gone to the Heavenly
Kingdom," she means that her mother is
(A) dead (B) in America (C) at Thornfield Hall
(D) asleep
7. When Jane says that the hall looks "like a corridor in
Bluebeard's castle," she means
(A) there are many weapons in the hall (B) there is
something terrible about the hall (C) the hall is cheerful
and well-lit (D) all corridors look the same
8. Which of the following is the most illogical part of the story?
(A) That Mr. Rochester is so rich (B) That Thornfield
Hall is so large and beautiful (C) That Adele does not
speak English well (D) That Mrs. Fairfax had not
mentioned Grace Poole before

IDENTIFYING THE MOOD
9. How does Jane feel after she meets Grace Poole?
(A) Happy (B) Afraid (C) Puzzled (D) Angry
10. Which of the following is most important at Thornfield Hall?
(A) Doing things quickly (B) Keeping everything in
order (C) Speaking in English only (D) Believing in
ghosts

THINKING IT OVER
1. In this chapter, Jane learns that there are two more people
who live at Thornfield Hall. Who are these people? Why do
you think Mrs. Fairfax had not mentioned them to Jane the
night before?

2. As they reach the third floor of the house, Mrs. Fairfax says to Jane, "If there were a ghost at Thornfield Hall, it would haunt this part of the house." Does this remind you of anything Jane said at the end of Chapter 1? What? Do you think Jane believes in ghosts? Explain your answers.

3. In the two paragraphs describing the attic, the staircase, and the hall of the third floor, the author emphasizes "narrowness" and "dimness." What feelings do you think the author is trying to suggest to the reader? What other words in the description suggest the same or similar feelings?

CHAPTER 3

FINDING THE MAIN IDEA

1. Which title tells most about the chapter?
   (A) "The Master Returns"   (B) "Strange Laughter"
   (C) "The Gytrash"   (D) "A Dull Time"

REMEMBERING DETAIL

2. Jane tries to talk with Grace Poole, but Grace
   (A) starts to laugh   (B) calls her names   (C) doesn't say much   (D) can't hear well

3. Jane describes the traveler as being all of these EXCEPT
   (A) wide-chested   (B) stern-looking   (C) very tall
   (D) about thirty-five

4. Jane tells the traveler that
   (A) she is the governess   (B) her name is Jane Eyre
   (C) she is afraid of him   (D) she knows Mr. Rochester very well

DRAWING CONCLUSIONS

5. You can guess that Mr. Rochester (the traveler) does not like to
   (A) ride horses   (B) ask questions of other people
   (C) arrive early   (D) say much about himself

USING YOUR REASON

6. Which of the following is the most illogical part of the story?
   (A) Jane would walk all the way to Hay to mail a letter.
   (B) The traveler did not break his leg in the fall from his horse.   (C) The traveler asked Jane for help.   (D) The traveler did not tell Jane that he is Mr. Rochester.

IDENTIFYING THE MOOD

7. When Jane sees a human riding on the horse, she probably feels

(A) joy (B) relief (C) fear (D) sorrow

READING FOR DEEPER MEANING

8. Jane seems to realize that the traveler is a man who

(A) lies to people (B) is unsure of himself (C) is used to giving orders (D) would kill her if he didn't need help

THINKING IT OVER

1. By now you know a little more about Jane. Tell what you know. For example, what does Jane say about her age? What about her character? Is she curious, or is she shy? What makes you think so?

2. There are two times in the chapter when Jane is afraid: when she sees the "Gytrash" coming, and when she tries to get hold of the horse. How does Jane act in the face of her fear? What does this tell you about her character?

3. What do you learn about the personality of the traveler? Why do you think he does not tell Jane that he is Mr. Rochester?

CHAPTER 4

FINDING THE MAIN IDEA

1. This chapter is mostly about

(A) the dog, Pilot (B) Jane's little pupil, Adele
(C) Jane's drawings and paintings (D) Jane's conversation with Mr. Rochester

REMEMBERING DETAIL

2. All of the following are true about Jane EXCEPT

(A) she is eighteen years old (B) her only relative is an uncle (C) she has lived in a charity school (D) she lived with her parents until she was fourteen

3. Jane thinks that Mr. Rochester is

(A) cruel and stupid (B) changeable and abrupt
(C) carefree and lighthearted (D) generous and loving

4. What does Jane learn about Mr. Rochester?

(A) He has painful thoughts. (B) He is really a happy man. (C) His family used to be poor. (D) He loved his brother very much.

DRAWING CONCLUSIONS

5. You can tell that Mr. Rochester thinks that Jane
   (A) has had an exciting life   (B) has no pride in herself
   (C) is a better artist than pianist   (D) is a poor teacher
   for Adele

USING YOUR REASON

6. When Mr. Rochester says that Jane has "lived the life of a
   nun," he means she
   (A) has been a nun for most of her life   (B) is a very
   religious person   (C) has had little contact with the world
   (D) has no family

7. The most illogical part of Mr. Rochester's talk with Jane is
   the part about
   (A) Jane's past life   (B) fairies and fairy tales   (C) Jane's
   sketches and paintings   (D) Adele's progress as a student

IDENTIFYING THE MOOD

8. Which of the following best describes Mr. Rochester's
   character?
   (A) Forceful   (B) Cowardly   (C) Relaxed   (D) Evil

READING FOR DEEPER MEANING

9. Jane's responses to Mr. Rochester show her feelings of
   (A) love for him   (B) disrespect for him   (C) anger
   with herself   (D) confidence in herself

THINKING IT OVER

1. The conversation between Mr. Rochester and Jane can be
   seen as a "match of wits." It is almost as if Mr. Rochester
   is testing Jane. What do you think he learns about Jane's
   character from her responses? Which of Jane's responses do
   you think show her character? What do Mr. Rochester's
   questions and remarks show about him?

2. At the end of the chapter, Mrs. Fairfax tells Jane more
   about Mr. Rochester. How does Mrs. Fairfax explain Mr.
   Rochester's behavior to Jane?

3. Mrs. Fairfax also says, "Perhaps he (Mr. Rochester) has still
   other reasons for avoiding the old place (Thornfield Hall)."
   What do you think these reasons might be?

CHAPTER 5

FINDING THE MAIN IDEA

1. Which title tells most about the chapter?
   (A) "Jane's Little Lie"   (B) "Presents for Adele"
   (C) "Mr. Rochester's Confession"   (D) "The Chatter of Children"

REMEMBERING DETAIL

2. Mr. Rochester asks Jane to give him
   (A) her honest opinions   (B) her hand in marriage
   (C) thirty pounds a year   (D) a few of her books
3. Jane thinks that Mr. Rochester is
   (A) a born liar   (B) a happy man   (C) a very handsome man   (D) an attractive man
4. Mr. Rochester admits that he has
   (A) many faults   (B) no regrets about his life   (C) killed his brother   (D) been hated by many people

DRAWING CONCLUSIONS

5. You can guess that Mr. Rochester
   (A) cares deeply for Mrs. Fairfax   (B) enjoys the company of children   (C) thinks highly of Jane   (D) would rather not talk to Jane

USING YOUR REASON

6. When Mr. Rochester says Jane "speaks like a lawyer," he means
   (A) her statements are direct and to the point   (B) her statements are long and boring   (C) she is interested only in money   (D) she should have become a lawyer
7. Mr. Rochester wants to talk with Jane because he believes she is
   (A) secretly in love with him   (B) a sympathetic listener
   (C) interested in his sinful life   (D) the only person that cares for him

IDENTIFYING THE MOOD

8. How does Jane feel after she has told Mr. Rochester that she does not think he is handsome?
   (A) Scornful   (B) Embarrassed   (C) Self-righteous
   (D) Frightened

9. At the end of the chapter, Mr. Rochester feels
   (A) angry   (B) optimistic   (C) foolish   (D) unhappy

READING FOR DEEPER MEANING

10. The chapter suggests that a happy life requires
    (A) a happy marriage   (B) a few sinful pleasures
    (C) correct thoughts and actions   (D) the admiration of
    one's employees

THINKING IT OVER

1. This chapter, like the one before it, is mostly a conversation
   between Jane and Mr. Rochester. How is the conversation in
   chapter 5 different from the one in chapter 4? How is it
   similar? Explain your answers.

2. At one point, Jane says to Mr. Rochester that "no free-born
   person would give up the right to speak an honest opinion,
   even for a salary." What is Mr. Rochester's answer to this?
   Do you agree with him? Why or why not?

3. Jane says that Mr. Rochester is not handsome. But later she
   says, "There was some power about him which made him
   attractive—especially to me." Is Jane contradicting herself?
   Why or why not?

CHAPTER 6

FINDING THE MAIN IDEA

1. Which title tells most about the chapter?
   (A) "Waves of Joy"   (B) "A Fire at Night"   (C) "A
   Noise in the Corridor"   (D) "Mr. Rochester's Wicked
   Life"

REMEMBERING DETAIL

2. Jane learns from Mr. Rochester about his
   (A) wicked life   (B) father's riches   (C) brother's death
   (D) relationship to Mrs. Fairfax' husband

3. Where is the fire mainly located?
   (A) In the corridor   (B) In Jane's room   (C) On the
   third floor   (D) Around Mr. Rochester's bed

4. After Jane puts out the fire, Mr. Rochester tells her that
   (A) she must wake up all the servants   (B) she must say
   nothing about the fire   (C) he will spend the rest of the
   night in the kitchen   (D) Grace Poole did not set the fire

DRAWING CONCLUSIONS

5. You can tell from the chapter that Jane and Mr. Rochester
   (A) distrust each other   (B) are annoyed at each other
   (C) are attracted to each other   (D) don't care much about
   each other

USING YOUR REASON

6. A person of "high character" is most likely a person who
   (A) likes to get "high"   (B) lives a decent life   (C) refuses
   to repay debts   (D) would kick someone who is down
7. Mr. Rochester goes to the third floor to
   (A) see how much damage the fire caused   (B) see if Jane
   will follow him   (C) spy on Jane from the window
   (D) find out who started the fire

IDENTIFYING THE MOOD

8. At the end of the chapter, Mr. Rochester seems to be
   (A) ready to commit suicide   (B) calm and relaxed
   (C) in love with Jane   (D) afraid that Jane will quit

READING FOR DEEPER MEANING

9. The chapter suggests that misfortune can
   (A) happen only to the wealthy   (B) make fools of the
   wise   (C) make a good person lead a bad life   (D) happen
   only to those who look for it

THINKING IT OVER

1. Mr. Rochester thanks Jane for saving his life. He says he is in
   her debt, but that he feels "no burden" in a debt to Jane.
   What does he mean by this? What does this show about his
   feelings for Jane?
2. In the last sentence in the chapter, Jane says, "Till morning
   dawned I was tossed on a sea where billows of trouble rolled
   under waves of joy." What trouble is Jane talking about?
   What joy?
3. How do you think the fire started? Has someone really tried
   to kill Mr. Rochester? Explain your answers.

CHAPTER 7

FINDING THE MAIN IDEA

1. In this chapter, the author is most interested in telling about

(A) Grace Poole's conversation with Jane   (B) the servant's reaction to the fire   (C) Jane's feelings for Mr. Rochester
(D) Mr. Rochester's love for Blanche Ingram

REMEMBERING DETAIL

2. The servants think the fire started when
   (A) Grace Poole set it   (B) Pilot kicked over a candle in the hallway   (C) some burning embers flew out of the fireplace   (D) Mr. Rochester fell asleep with his candle lit
3. During her conversation with Grace Poole, Jane realizes that Grace
   (A) did not set the fire   (B) is in love with Mr. Rochester
   (C) is hiding a knife in her pocket   (D) is trying to get information from her
4. When did Mr. Rochester leave Thornfield Hall?
   (A) Right after the fire   (B) Right after breakfast
   (C) Just before dinner   (D) At six in the evening

DRAWING CONCLUSIONS

5. You can guess that Mr. Rochester has gone to see his friends particularly because he
   (A) enjoys singing duets   (B) is tired of Thornfield Hall
   (C) has some business to discuss   (D) wants to see Blanche Ingram

USING YOUR REASON

6. Jane is amazed by Grace Poole's self-possession. If you had "self-possession," you probably would
   (A) stay calm during times of danger   (B) set a fire when you get angry   (C) lose control of your emotions   (D) not give help during an emergency
7. Jane's reason for speaking with Grace Poole is to
   (A) find out where Mr. Rochester is   (B) become better acquainted with her   (C) see if Grace will appear guilty
   (D) offer her help in sewing the curtains

IDENTIFYING THE MOOD

8. How does Jane feel when she finds out where Mr. Rochester has gone?
   (A) Jealous   (B) Hopeful   (C) Greedy   (D) Terrified

READING FOR DEEPER MEANING

9. It seems that in the world of *Jane Eyre,* women are most
   admired for their
   (A) beauty   (B) intelligence   (C) wealth   (D) kindness

THINKING IT OVER

1. Jane thinks Mr. Rochester is protecting Grace Poole. Why do
   you think he might do so? What kind of "hold" do you think
   Grace Poole might have on him?
2. Grace Poole remains very calm during her conversation with
   Jane. What do you think this might tell about Grace Poole?
3. At the end of the chapter, Jane decides to make two pictures.
   What are these pictures of? Why does Jane want to make
   them? What does this show about Jane's ability to accept
   disappointment?

CHAPTER 8

FINDING THE MAIN IDEA

1. Which title tells most about the chapter?
   (A) "A Letter from Mr. Rochester"   (B) "A Duet in the
   Drawing Room"   (C) "A Beautiful and Haughty Lady"
   (D) "A Quiet Corner"

REMEMBERING DETAIL

2. Mr. Rochester's letter says he will be arriving with his guests
   in
   (A) two hours   (B) three days   (C) six days
   (D) two weeks
3. Blanche Ingram's laugh is full of
   (A) joy and merriment   (B) shyness and love
   (C) silliness and insincerity   (D) scorn and sarcasm
4. When Jane leaves the drawing room, she is followed by
   (A) Mrs. Dent   (B) Blanche Ingram   (C) Adele and
   Sophie   (D) Mr. Rochester

DRAWING CONCLUSIONS

5. You can guess that while Mr. Rochester was away, he has
   (A) missed Jane   (B) gotten sick   (C) not enjoyed himself
   (D) asked Blanche Ingram to marry him

USING YOUR REASON

6. When Jane says that Blanche Ingram is "on her high horse," she means that Blanche is
   (A) conceited   (B) humorous   (C) embarrassed
   (D) close-mouthed

7. The real reason Jane leaves the drawing room early is that she
   (A) is bored with the music   (B) feels out of place
   (C) is angry with Blanche Ingram   (D) doesn't want to disturb Mr. Rochester

IDENTIFYING THE MOOD

8. Jane feels best about the fact that Mr. Rochester is
   (A) separated from her by rank and wealth   (B) not so handsome as the other young men   (C) bound to her in mind and heart   (D) paying a lot of attention to Blanche Ingram

READING FOR DEEPER MEANING

9. According to Blanche Ingram, which of the following is most important in a man?
   (A) Courage   (B) Looks   (C) Profession   (D) Self-love

THINKING IT OVER

1. In this chapter, you get some idea of how wealthy people lived at that time. How are their lives different from the lives of the servants? How are their lives similar to the lives of the servants?

2. Look again at the long discussion on governesses. The Ingrams don't seem to care that Jane overhears them. What do you think this shows about the Ingrams?

3. Does the author want you to like Blanche Ingram? How can you tell?

CHAPTER 9

FINDING THE MAIN IDEA

1. Which title tells most about the chapter?
   (A) "A Dull Day"   (B) "Mr. Rochester Departs"
   (C) "Blanche Ingram's Fortune"   (D) "Two Unexpected Visitors"

REMEMBERING DETAIL

2. Where is the home of the newcomer, Mr. Mason?
   (A) America   (B) Spain   (C) The West Indies
   (D) Thornfield Hall
3. The Gypsy wants to see
   (A) Mr. Rochester   (B) Colonel Dent and Mr. Mason
   (C) young, single women   (D) everyone in the house
4. Blanche Ingram learns from the Gypsy that Mr. Rochester
   (A) will ask her to marry him   (B) will marry no one
   among the women at Thornfield Hall   (C) is secretly in love
   with Jane   (D) is not as wealthy as Blanche thought

USING YOUR REASON

5. When the Gypsy speaks to Jane of "the fire that is in you,"
   the Gypsy means the feeling of
   (A) pain   (B) love   (C) anger   (D) revenge
6. The reason Mr. Rochester disguises himself is to
   (A) find out the true feelings of Blanche Ingram and Jane
   (B) provide some entertainment for his guests   (C) discover
   who has been stealing his wine   (D) learn why Mr. Mason
   has come

DRAWING CONCLUSIONS

7. You can tell from the chapter that Mr. Rochester
   (A) knew that Mr. Mason was coming to Thornfield Hall
   (B) cares for Jane above all the others   (C) is happy that
   Blanche Ingram loves him   (D) is sorry that Jane came to
   Thornfield Hall

IDENTIFYING THE MOOD

8. When Mr. Rochester learns that Mr. Mason has arrived,
   Rochester is
   (A) upset   (B) furious   (C) joyous   (D) uncaring

READING FOR DEEPER MEANING

9. The chapter suggests that in order to get happiness, you
   should
   (A) work hard   (B) sit and dream   (C) reach out for it
   (D) wait for it to come

THINKING IT OVER

1. In this chapter, the character of Blanche Ingram is clearly shown. What is she really like? How can you tell? How does she act toward Jane? Why do you think she acts this way?
2. What does Mr. Rochester say to Jane that indicates his feelings for her? What are his feelings for her?
3. What does the Gypsy (Rochester) say about Grace Poole? Do you believe him? Why or why not?
4. Whom do you think this mysterious Mr. Mason might be? Does Rochester say anything that might indicate why Mason has come? If so, what?

CHAPTER 10

FINDING THE MAIN IDEA

1. The author is mostly interested in telling how
   (A) Mr. Rochester's guests are awakened by a cry
   (B) Jane's love for Mr. Rochester grows   (C) the mystery at Thornfield Hall deepens   (D) Mr. Mason leaves Thornfield Hall

REMEMBERING DETAIL

2. The cry and sounds of a struggle come from
   (A) the corridor   (B) Blanche Ingram's room   (C) the stairway to the attic   (D) the room just above Jane's
3. Rochester explains the cry by saying
   (A) Mr. Mason injured himself   (B) a fire broke out in the attic   (C) a servant had a nightmare   (D) the dog attacked a robber
4. Mr. Mason's wounds are from a
   (A) woman's bite   (B) robber's knife   (C) tiger's claws
   (D) gunshot

DRAWING CONCLUSIONS

5. You can guess that Rochester forbids Jane and Mason to speak to each other because
   (A) someone may overhear them   (B) Mason's wounds may get worse   (C) Mason may give away Rochester's secret
   (D) Jane wouldn't understand what Mason is talking about

USING YOUR REASON

6. When Mr. Rochester says, "I am like a man who has built his house on the edge of a volcano," he means
(A) he is a very foolish man   (B) he is always in danger
(C) he is not afraid of anything   (D) Thornfield Hall is built on the edge of a volcano

7. Which of the following is the most illogical part of the chapter?
(A) That all of the guests would be awakened by the cry
(B) That Jane would be sent for a sponge and smelling salts
(C) That Mr. Mason would agree to say nothing about what happened   (D) That Mr. Rochester would lock the door to the mysterious room

IDENTIFYING THE MOOD

8. Which word best describes how Mr. Mason feels when he leaves Thornfield Hall?
(A) Calm   (B) Sad   (C) Angry   (D) Bitter

READING FOR DEEPER MEANING

9. Jane believes that breaking the law
(A) can never be good   (B) can be good if it is done for the right reason   (C) is all right if no one is hurt   (D) is all right

THINKING IT OVER

1. The relationship between Mr. Rochester and Mr. Mason is hard to understand. At first, Mr. Rochester seems afraid of Mr. Mason. Later, Mr. Rochester commands Mr. Mason and Mr. Mason obeys. Whom do you think Mr. Mason is? Why has he come to Thornfield Hall?

2. Mr. Rochester says, "There is a shameful thing which I keep locked up in that house." Mr. Mason says, "Let her be treated as tenderly as may be." What do you think is in the mysterious room?

3. At the end of the chapter, Mr. Rochester and Jane discuss breaking the law. What does each say about it? Whom do you agree with? Explain your answers.

4. Look back to earlier parts of *Jane Eyre* to see if you can find any idea of what the mystery may be about. Tell what you find.

CHAPTER 11

FINDING THE MAIN IDEA

1. Which title tells most about the chapter?
   (A) "A Proposal of Marriage"   (B) "The Old Chestnut Tree"   (C) "A Walk in the Garden"   (D) "A Storm at Night"

REMEMBERING DETAIL

2. When Jane first sees Mr. Rochester in the garden, she tries to
   (A) hit him   (B) surprise him   (C) avoid him
   (D) propose to him
3. Mr. Rochester first tells Jane that
   (A) she has been very cruel to him   (B) she will have to leave Thornfield Hall   (C) he will go to visit her in Ireland
   (D) he is already married to Blanche Ingram
4. After Jane agrees to marry him, Mr. Rochester
   (A) begins to jump for joy   (B) makes a very strange statement   (C) strikes the chestnut tree with his fist
   (D) sits in the garden till morning

DRAWING CONCLUSIONS

5. You can guess that Mr. Rochester
   (A) doesn't believe that Jane loves him   (B) would prefer to marry Blanche Ingram   (C) is worried about what will happen to Adele   (D) knows that marrying Jane will lead to problems

USING YOUR REASON

6. When Mr. Rochester says, "As for man's opinion—I wash my hands of it," he means that he
   (A) likes clean hands   (B) has no opinions of his own
   (C) doesn't care what other people think   (D) is worried about what other people will say
7. Mr. Rochester's reason for tricking Jane into believing that he will marry Blanche Ingram is to
   (A) get Jane to leave Thornfield Hall   (B) make Jane feel stupid   (C) make Jane show her feelings for him
   (D) show Jane that he doesn't care for her

IDENTIFYING THE MOOD

8. In talking with Mr. Rochester, Jane experiences all of these feelings EXCEPT

(A) sorrow (B) happiness (C) doubt (D) hate

THINKING IT OVER

1. Do you think it was necessary for Mr. Rochester to trick Jane? Why? How else might he have "awakened her feelings"?
2. Jane and Mr. Rochester seem to be happy at their decision to marry. But does the chapter end on a happy note? How does the chapter end? What might the ending represent?

CHAPTER 12

FINDING THE MAIN IDEA

1. In this chapter the author is mostly interested in telling about (A) Mr. Rochester's surprise gift for Jane (B) the preparations for the wedding (C) the fearful night that Jane has spent (D) Jane's long wait for Mr. Rochester to return

REMEMBERING DETAIL

2. Jane dreams that she and Mr. Rochester
(A) die suddenly (B) part forever (C) come to hate each other (D) marry and live happily
3. In the morning, Jane finds
(A) wilted flowers (B) blood on the carpet (C) a broken window (D) a ripped veil
4. Mr. Rochester explains that the visitor in Jane's room was
(A) an unknown woman (B) a vampire (C) Sophie (D) Grace Poole

DRAWING CONCLUSIONS

5. You can guess that the reason the visitor went to Jane's room was because she
(A) was Mr. Rochester in another disguise (B) came to Jane's room by mistake (C) was probably playing a joke on Jane (D) did not want Jane and Mr. Rochester to marry

USING YOUR REASON

6. Which of these is the best example of a "mental terror"?
   (A) A nightmare   (B) A poem   (C) A fire   (D) A conversation

7. Why does Mr. Rochester keep Grace Poole in his house?
   (A) Mr. Rochester doesn't say.   (B) She is his sister.
   (C) She has once saved his life.   (D) She has always lived there.

IDENTIFYING THE MOOD

8. How does Jane feel after she hears Mr. Rochester's explanation?
   (A) Relieved   (B) Frightened   (C) Guilty
   (D) Sorrowful

THINKING IT OVER

1. If you were to wake up from a bad dream and you were to see someone strange in your room, what would you do? Would you do what Jane did? Why or why not?

2. Jane says the mysterious, savage-looking woman in her room was not Grace Poole. Mr. Rochester says it was. Who do you believe? If it wasn't Grace Poole or anyone else who Jane knew, then who do you think it might have been? Explain your answers.

3. Think back to earlier chapters. Can you recall anything that might give a clue to this mystery? Tell about it.

CHAPTER 13

FINDING THE MAIN IDEA

1. Which title tells most about the chapter?
   (A) "Mr. Rochester's Wife"   (B) "The Wedding in the Church"   (C) "Nurse Poole"   (D) "Jane's Uncle"

REMEMBERING DETAIL

2. Who interrupts the wedding ceremony?
   (A) Grace Poole   (B) A clerk named Green   (C) A lawyer named Briggs   (D) Bertha Antoinetta Mason

3. Mr. Rochester's wife is all of the following EXCEPT
   (A) a lunatic   (B) a drunkard   (C) Mr. Mason's sister
   (D) Grace Poole

4. What does Jane learn about her uncle?
(A) He is dying. (B) He is coming to England. (C) He has found Jane's mother. (D) He is related to Mr. Rochester.

DRAWING CONCLUSIONS
5. You can guess that Mr. Rochester's wife
(A) is happy to see her brother (B) loves her husband very much (C) would like to apologize for her behavior (D) is the person who set the fire

USING YOUR REASON
6. When Jane says that Mr. Rochester's "face was hard as rock," she means
(A) he is crying (B) he is smiling (C) he is upset (D) he is happy
7. Mr. Rochester believes it is all right for him to marry Jane because
(A) he is legally divorced from Bertha (B) Bertha is not a "true partner" in marriage (C) he and Bertha have no children (D) Bertha has no money

IDENTIFYING THE MOOD
8. Which word best describes Mr. Rochester's feelings after his fight with Bertha?
(A) Bitter (B) Glad (C) Calm (D) Sentimental

READING FOR DEEPER MEANING
9. At the time of *Jane Eyre,* what did people probably believe about insanity?
(A) It could be cured. (B) It was very shameful. (C) It happened only to women. (D) It happened only after marriage.

THINKING IT OVER
1. At last the mystery of Thornfield Hall is revealed. Why do you suppose Mr. Rochester married Bertha? Are there any clues in this or previous chapters? (See the end of Chapter 4.)
2. Do you think Mr. Rochester is right in trying to marry Jane? Why or why not?
3. What is sarcasm? What does Mr. Rochester really mean when he refers to Bertha as a "precious jewel of a wife"?

Are there any other instances of Mr. Rochester's sarcasm in this chapter? What are they?

CHAPTER 14

FINDING THE MAIN IDEA

1. The author is mostly interested in telling how
(A) Jane leaves Thornfield Hall   (B) Mr. Rochester asks Jane to forgive him   (C) Bertha Mason became insane (D) Mr. Rochester almost commits suicide

REMEMBERING DETAIL

2. When Mr. Rochester asks Jane to forgive him, Jane
(A) forgives him completely but is unable to say it
(B) tells him truthfully that she forgives him   (C) lies and says that she forgives him   (D) tells him that she will never forgive him
3. Mr. Rochester says that his father
(A) didn't care at all about money   (B) wanted to be known as a good, kind man   (C) divided his fortune between his sons   (D) knew that there was insanity in the Mason family
4. Who sees Jane leaving Thornfield Hall?
(A) No one   (B) Mr. Rochester   (C) Adele   (D) Mrs. Fairfax

DRAWING CONCLUSIONS

5. You can tell from the chapter that Mr. Rochester still
(A) hopes that Bertha can be cured   (B) is angry at his father and brother   (C) wishes he were living in the West Indies   (D) believes that beauty is important in a woman

USING YOUR REASON

6. When Mr. Rochester speaks of what is in a woman's "heart and mind," he means her
(A) beauty   (B) health   (C) character   (D) wealth
7. Jane's reason for leaving Thornfield Hall is that
(A) Mr. Rochester no longer cares for her   (B) she is afraid of what Bertha might do   (C) Mr. Rochester is legally married to Bertha   (D) she would rather teach at a school

IDENTIFYING THE MOOD

8. As Jane leaves Thornfield Hall, she feels sad and
   (A) angry   (B) hopeless   (C) frightened   (D) puzzled

READING FOR DEEPER MEANING

9. In the world of *Jane Eyre,* which of the following was probably true about divorce?
   (A) It was completely illegal.   (B) It was legal and very common.   (C) It was legal only if one of the partners was insane.   (D) It was legal but not approved of.

THINKING IT OVER

1. Mr. Rochester says that his father considered Bertha Mason "a good match" for him. What do you think Mr. Rochester's father meant by this? What would you consider a "good match"?
2. What feelings do you think Mr. Rochester has toward his father and brother? Why do you think so?
3. Why do you think Mr. Rochester did not get a divorce? What reasons does the chapter imply?
4. Do you think Jane is doing the right thing by leaving? Why or why not? What would you do if you were Jane?

CHAPTER 15

FINDING THE MAIN IDEA

1. This chapter is mostly about
   (A) Jane's young students   (B) Jane's memories of Mr. Rochester   (C) two new people whom Jane meets   (D) the rich man who pays for the school

REMEMBERING DETAIL

2. By what name does Jane call herself?
   (A) Jane Rochester   (B) Adele Eyre   (C) Rosamond Oliver   (D) Jane Elliot
3. The parson, Mr. Rivers, tells Jane that he
   (A) knows all about Jane's past   (B) thinks a priest's life is exciting   (C) is in love with Rosamond Oliver   (D) will become a missionary in India
4. Rosamond Oliver asks St. John Rivers to
   (A) come visit her father   (B) let her teach the schoolgirls

(C) join the Seventh Regiment   (D) bring Jane to Vale
Hall

DRAWING CONCLUSIONS
5. You can guess that Rosamond Oliver
(A) wants to marry a rich man   (B) is attracted to St. John
Rivers   (C) has had a very difficult life   (D) doesn't want
anything to do with Jane

USING YOUR REASON
6. When Rosamond says to St. John, "You are quite a stranger
at Vale Hall," she means
(A) nobody knows him at Vale Hall   (B) he seldom comes
to visit anymore   (C) he is a strange man   (D) nobody
cares about him at Vale Hall
7. Jane's main reason for changing her name is that she
(A) doesn't want her old friends to find her   (B) believes
that a new name means good luck   (C) had never known
her parents, so her name doesn't matter   (D) had never
liked the name Jane Eyre

IDENTIFYING THE MOOD
8. Which of the following best describes Rosamond's attitude
toward Jane?
(A) Rude   (B) Scornful   (C) Friendly   (D) Pitying

READING FOR DEEPER MEANING
9. You can see from what St. John says that he thinks which
of the following is a good way to be?
(A) Self-pitying   (B) Forward-looking   (C) Curious
(D) Content

THINKING IT OVER
1. How does Jane describe the girls she teaches? What does
Jane say about their "flesh and blood"? Do you think this
attitude was a common one at the time of *Jane Eyre?* Is
this attitude a common one today? Explain your answers.
2. What does Jane observe about St. John's feelings for Rosamond? Why do you think he acts the way he does toward
Rosamond?
3. What do you think are Rosamond's feelings toward St. John?
How can you tell? How does Rosamond try to make him
jealous? Do you think she succeeds? Explain your answers.

CHAPTER 16

FINDING THE MAIN IDEA
1. The chapter is mostly about
(A) Rosamond's visits to Jane   (B) St. John's feelings for
Rosamond   (C) Jane's students and how much they like
her   (D) St. John's quick exit from Jane's cottage

REMEMBERING DETAIL
2. Rosamond usually comes to visit the school when
(A) the students are having lunch   (B) St. John is giving a
lesson   (C) Jane is teaching sewing   (D) the students are
doing arithmetic
3. What does St. John say about Rosamond?
(A) She is spoiled and selfish.   (B) She would enjoy living
in India.   (C) He loves her.   (D) He wants to marry her.
4. What does St. John take from Jane's cottage?
(A) A small piece of wood   (B) Two of Jane's brushes
(C) The drawing of Rosamond   (D) A scrap of paper

DRAWING CONCLUSIONS
5. You can tell that St. John thinks that
(A) all women are silly   (B) Jane's drawing of Rosamond
is not good   (C) Rosamond's love for him is not serious
(D) Rosamond will be heartbroken when he leaves

USING YOUR REASON
6. Jane describes Rosamond's "purple riding habit." In this
sentence, the word "habit" means
(A) a kind of horse   (B) a type of clothing   (C) any
purple-colored object   (D) something a person does all the
time
7. What is St. John's reason for not marrying Rosamond?
(A) Rosamond would not like the life of a missionary.
(B) Rosamond needs to learn about disappointment and
sorrow.   (C) Poor men cannot marry rich women.
(D) A parson may not marry.

IDENTIFYING THE MOOD
8. As St. John leaves Jane's house, it seems as if he feels
(A) jolly   (B) tired   (C) foolish   (D) excited

READING FOR DEEPER MEANING

9. Which of the following is most important for St. John?
   (A) Work   (B) Love   (C) Art   (D) Health

THINKING IT OVER

1. Rosamond is described as a rich and beautiful young woman. So was Blanche Ingram. In what other ways are they similar? In what ways are they different?
2. How would you describe the character of St. John Rivers? What kind of person would give up the chance for love in order to continue his or her work? Do you know anyone like this? Tell about him or her.
3. What do you think Mr. Rochester is doing during all this time? Do you think his part in the book is finished? Explain your answers.

CHAPTER 17

FINDING THE MAIN IDEA

1. Which title tells most about the chapter?
   (A) "A Chance to Go to India"   (B) "The Scrap of Paper"
   (C) "A Winter Evening"   (D) "Messages from Afar"

REMEMBERING DETAIL

2. Jane learns that her dead uncle has left her
   (A) two thousand pounds   (B) his house in London
   (C) his crystal goblets   (D) twenty thousand pounds
3. What does St. John ask Jane to do?
   (A) Wait for him   (B) Lend him some money   (C) Marry him and go to India   (D) Take a message to Rosamond
4. Whose voice does Jane hear calling?
   (A) Mr. Rochester's   (B) Rosamond's   (C) St. John's
   (D) Her mother's

DRAWING CONCLUSIONS

5. You can guess that great wealth will
   (A) spoil Jane's good nature   (B) make Jane unhappy
   (C) not change Jane much   (D) make Jane like Blanche Ingram

USING YOUR REASON

6. When Jane mentions "the game of Fate," she means the
(A) life of a missionary   (B) chances that turn up in one's
life   (C) card game she is playing with St. John   (D) problems of being a school teacher

7. Jane is not immediately happy about her new riches because she
(A) realizes that she has no relatives   (B) knows what
money has done to Mr. Rochester   (C) realizes she will
have to leave her students   (D) doesn't want the independence money will give her

IDENTIFYING THE MOOD

8. During the "amazing happening" at the end of the chapter, Jane feels
(A) happy and playful   (B) puzzled and sad   (C) powerful and alert   (D) mischievous and silly

READING FOR DEEPER MEANING

9. The author would most agree with which of the following?
(A) Women must be obedient to men.   (B) No honest
person ever became rich.   (C) Nature can work in strange
ways.   (D) Only fools fall in love.

THINKING IT OVER

1. What does Jane realize about St. John's proposal of marriage?
What are her thoughts and feelings about it? Do you think
it would be wise for her to marry him? Why or why not?

2. Do you think Jane really hears Mr. Rochester's voice, or is
she just imagining it? What makes you say so? Assuming that
she really has heard it, what explanation would you give for
this strange event?

CHAPTER 18

FINDING THE MAIN IDEA

1. The author is mostly interested in telling
(A) how Bertha died   (B) what Jane sees at Thornfield
Hall   (C) what has happened to Mr. Rochester   (D) how
the servants escaped from the fire

REMEMBERING DETAIL

2. When did Thornfield Hall burn down?
   (A) In late January   (B) On a Sunday afternoon
   (C) The night before Jane got back   (D) Two months after Jane left

3. How did Bertha die?
   (A) She stabbed herself.   (B) She jumped from the roof.
   (C) She was overcome by smoke.   (D) Mr. Rochester killed her.

4. Mr. Rochester is now living
   (A) in the city of London   (B) at a farm called Ferndean
   (C) in a small house behind Thornfield Hall   (D) at the inn called The Rochester Arms

DRAWING CONCLUSIONS

5. The chapter suggests that when the fire broke out, Grace Poole was
   (A) drunk and sound asleep   (B) away on vacation
   (C) sitting in Jane's old room   (D) in the kitchen with Mrs. Fairfax

USING YOUR REASON

6. When the inn keeper says that Mr. Rochester is a "fixture," he means that Mr. Rochester
   (A) is now in jail   (B) has a job fixing things   (C) is locked up in a madhouse   (D) cannot move around very easily

7. To "amputate" means to
   (A) burn   (B) crush   (C) cut off   (D) make blind

8. The inn keeper pities Mr. Rochester mainly because Mr. Rochester
   (A) has lost Thornfield Hall   (B) is living in England
   (C) has lost his wife   (D) is blind and crippled

IDENTIFYING THE MOOD

9. How does Jane feel when she sees the ruins of Thornfield Hall?
   (A) Joyful   (B) Calm   (C) Sad   (D) Horrified

READING FOR DEEPER MEANING

10. The author would most agree with which of the following?
    (A) Mr. Rochester's injuries resulted from his courage and

kindness. (B) Mr. Rochester got exactly what he deserved.
(C) Jane is to blame for all that has happened. (D) Jane
would be wiser to return to the village of Morton.

THINKING IT OVER
1. When Jane thought she heard Mr. Rochester's voice, she
   described it as if it were full of "pain and sorrow." What does
   Jane learn in this chapter to show that her description is
   correct?
2. According to the innkeeper, some people say that Mr.
   Rochester's fate is "a just judgment on him." What do they
   mean by this? Do you agree? Why or why not?
3. Why would Mr. Rochester try to save his wife? What does
   this tell about the kind of person he is?
4. What is irony? Why is it "ironic" that Mr. Rochester would
   be injured while trying to save Bertha?

CHAPTER 19

FINDING THE MAIN IDEA
1. Which title tells most about the chapter?
   (A) "A Sad, Sad Story" (B) "The Farm at Ferndean"
   (C) "John and Mary" (D) "With Him Once Again"

REMEMBERING DETAIL
2. When does Jane reach Ferndean?
   (A) Late in the evening (B) Early in the morning (C) At
   midafternoon (D) Just before lunchtime
3. When he learns about St. John Rivers, Mr. Rochester tells
   Jane to
   (A) marry St. John (B) leave Ferndean immediately
   (C) forget about St. John (D) return to Thornfield Hall
4. Jane tells Mr. Rochester that she
   (A) has no money at all (B) wants to be his wife
   (C) cannot marry a blind man (D) will pay to rebuild
   Thornfield Hall

DRAWING CONCLUSIONS
5. You can tell that in the weeks before Jane's arrival, Mr.
   Rochester has
   (A) tried to kill himself (B) done a lot of traveling in

Europe   (C) enjoyed the company of many guests
(D) wanted to be left alone

USING YOUR REASON

6. When Mr. Rochester says, "What sweet madness has come over me," he means
(A) insanity is a good feeling   (B) he is both happy and angry   (C) he is unbelievably happy   (D) he has finally gone insane
7. Mr. Rochester has been feeling bad about himself because he
(A) heard Jane calling to him   (B) has given up his wicked habits   (C) has not done anything to help others   (D) will not get the chance to travel in Europe

IDENTIFYING THE MOOD

8. The overall tone of the chapter is one of
(A) sorrow   (B) anger   (C) joy   (D) humor

READING FOR DEEPER MEANING

9. The chapter suggests that a main point of living is to
(A) leave people alone   (B) enjoy yourself   (C) get a good job   (D) help other people

THINKING IT OVER

1. Mr. Rochester says that while he has done nothing wicked, he has also done nothing good. Do you think Mr. Rochester is correct about himself? Can you think of anything he has done that was good? Explain your answers.
2. Jane and Mr. Rochester are sure that they somehow communicated a few nights before. Why are they so sure? What does Jane mean when she says "surely our marriage is favored on earth and in heaven"? Why do you think she is so sure?

CHAPTER 20

FINDING THE MAIN IDEA

1. Which title tells most about the chapter?
(A) "Our Son Is Born"   (B) "Adele Grows Up"
(C) "Our Life Together"   (D) "St. John Goes to India"

REMEMBERING DETAIL

2. Jane is about what age at the time of this chapter?
   (A) Twenty   (B) Thirty   (C) Forty   (D) Fifty
3. How long was it before Mr. Rochester regained some vision?
   (A) Six months   (B) One year   (C) Two years
   (D) Ten years
4. What has Mr. Rochester mainly been doing since the marriage?
   (A) Writing books   (B) Working to help others
   (C) Tending a small garden   (D) Very little

DRAWING CONCLUSIONS

5. You can tell from the chapter that Mr. Rochester's blindness has
   (A) not affected his happiness   (B) made him bitter and angry   (C) made him unable to do anything   (D) caused his son to be born blind

USING YOUR REASON

6. By a "sound education," Jane means an education that
   (A) teaches a lot about music   (B) is for women only
   (C) is for rich students only   (D) covers all subjects well
7. The reason Jane and Mr. Rochester go to London is to
   (A) visit Adele   (B) speak with a doctor   (C) take a vacation   (D) say good-by to St. John Rivers
8. Which of the following best describes the character of Adele?
   (A) Pleasant   (B) Spoiled   (C) Serious   (D) Moody

9. Which of the following best describes the relationship between Jane and her husband?
   (A) Independent   (B) Uncommunicative   (C) Burdensome   (D) Sharing

THINKING IT OVER

1. Jane says that her husband "has helped to pass laws for the benefit of the working people and farmers of England. He has fought for the rights of all men." Would the Mr. Rochester of the early part of the book have done this? What has changed Mr. Rochester? Explain your answers.
2. In this last chapter, the author tells what happens to two

other characters in the book: Adele and St. John. What do you think has happened to Mrs. Fairfax? Grace Poole? Blanche Ingram? Rosamond Oliver? Why do you think the author has "forgotten" them in this last chapter? Are there any other people in the book whom you wonder about? Who are they? What do you think has happened to them?

3. Are you happy or unhappy with the way the book ends? What do you like about the ending? What don't you like? Tell why.